"WHAT?"

AY KING UCH ING HERE, BUT I'VE MADE THE DECISION TO JOIN YOUR DUCHY."

In Another World With My Smartphone 5

NOW COMMENCES THE DUCHY OF BRUNHILD'S FOUNDING CELEBRATION!!

I SPED THROUGH THE TREES LIKE A MADMAN, TAKING THE MITHRIL GREATSWORD OUT OF "STORAGE" AS I CHARGED. JUST IN TIME TO STOP HER FROM BEING IMPALED, I INTERCEPTED THE CREATURE'S LEG AND DEFLECTED IT AWAY FROM THE GIRL.

"GET TO SAFETY, FOCUS ON EVACUATING AND... YOU HAVE NO IDEA WHAT I'M SAYING, DO YOU?"

ONE YOUNG TRIBAL GIRL BARKED OUT WHAT SEEMED TO BE ORDERS, BUT I COULDN'T UNDERSTAND WHAT SHE WAS SAYING. IT WAS ODD TO ME THAT I DIDN'T UNDERSTAND HER, I HAD KIND OF JUST ASSUMED GOD HAD GIVEN ME AN OMNILINGUAL BODY OR SOMETHING.

"ACCEL BOOST!"

In Another World With My Smartphone

Patora Fuyuhara
illustration·Eiji Usatsuka

IN ANOTHER WORLD WITH MY SMARTPHONE: VOLUME 5
by Patora Fuyuhara

Translated by Andrew Hodgson
Edited by DxS

Original Japanese edition published in 2016 by Hobby Japan
This English edition is published by arrangement with Hobby Japan, Tokyo

English translation © 2018 J-Novel Club LLC

Find more books like this one at www.j-novel.club!

President and Publisher: Samuel Pinansky
Managing Editor: Aimee Zink

ISBN: 978-1-7183-5004-5
Printed in Korea
First Printing: August 2019
10 9 8 7 6 5 4 3 2 1

Contents

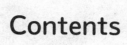

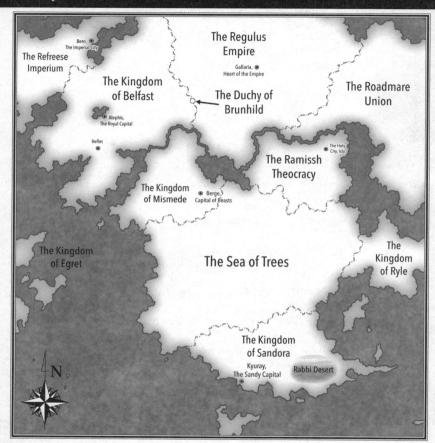

The Refreese Imperium

Bern, The Imperial City

The Regulus Empire

Gallaria, Heart of the Empire

The Kingdom of Belfast

Alephis, The Royal Capital

Reflet

The Duchy of Brunhild

The Roadmare Union

The Holy City, Isla

The Ramissh Theocracy

The Kingdom of Mismede

Berge, Capital of Beasts

The Kingdom of Egret

The Sea of Trees

The Kingdom of Ryle

The Kingdom of Sandora

Kyuray, The Sandy Capital

Rabbi Desert

N

The Story So Far!

This is the tale of Mochizuki Touya, a boy who was reborn into a new world, and took his Smartphone with him! After earning the support and backing of both the Kingdom of Belfast and the Regulus Empire, he founded a Duchy by the name of Brunhild, and gained the position of Grand Duke in the process. Using the power of Babylon, a relic of an ancient civilization, he was able to construct his own castle in no time at all. Plus, with three princesses by his side, he's slowly been building up a positive appearance of his Duchy to the outside world. With many precious partners to support him along the way, he has only just begun to take his first steps towards becoming a proper - if not a tad unconventional - Grand Duke.

Once, the two great powers of the continent's western sector were the Regulus Empire and the Kingdom of Belfast. Upon the border of these two nations, a new sovereign state was born. This new state was collaboratively backed by both superpowers.

The Duchy of Brunhild.

The territory of the state was minimal, composed of a tiny bit of land contributed by both larger nations. The grand duke who reigned over this territory was a man named Mochizuki Touya. He was a brave and mighty adventurer, one who had done the unprecedented. His rise to the guild's Silver Rank was the fastest in the history of the world.

Eventually, that man... and the name of his tiny nation, Brunhild, would have a far greater meaning in the context of world lore and history.

But that, dear listener, is a story yet to be told...

The three who had arrived to become the Duchy of Brunhild's first military agents were definitely skilled in the art of combat. It was no surprise, given that Leen had thought them worthy enough to bring.

Lain was skilled with a standard sword, Norn was a twinblade wielder, and Nikola wielded a halberd, which was a long hybrid of spear and axe. I had them demonstrate their skills against Yae, and they held their own fairly well. I was a little surprised, honestly.

"Milord, are there no horses within the castle grounds?"

"Horses?" Nikola brought up a fair point, which was starting to become habitual, and it made me realize that there were no horses in my little duchy. We got around using [Gate] mostly, so there was no need. And whenever we were back at Belfast's capital, I got around on a bike.

"Do we need horses?"

"I'd consider them a necessary part of any military cavalry. True, I don't expect to see combat any time soon, but it would be very valuable if we could have some to train how to fight on horseback."

That made sense. My soldiers were here to fight for me, so I probably had to spend a bit more time investing in their training.

Regulus and Belfast were on either side of Brunhild, so I wasn't really worried about seeing any military action... Still, there was no guarantee that bandits or rogues wouldn't appear in the nearby mountains or something.

"If we had horses we could begin patrolling the territory, and we'd also be able to chart and scout certain areas of interest in the region." Lain brought up another bonus to having some equine reinforcement.

Come to think of it, her voice really is boyish... Can I really be blamed for mistaking her for a man?! That aside, horses...

"I've got an idea, I'll summon you something way better than a horse."

"Pardon?" I ignored Nikola, who was now looking at me with a bewildered expression, and focused my magic on the ground.

"Come forth, Dark! I seek that which rules the skies, [Griffin]!" Once the smoke cleared, the magic circle vanished and a Griffin stood in its place.

"Whoa!"

"Incredible…"

"What is this?" The three of them reacted very differently, but their bewilderment was all the same. They simply stared at the Griffon before them.

"Well… you're, uh, Paul? No, you're John, right? Okay, John? From now on, you're Nikola's partner, got it? Please get along with each other."

"CAW!" John let out a small noise and trotted off to Nikola. Nikola seemed apprehensive at first, but tentatively reached out to pet John on the head, then on the back.

"Wow, he seems pretty obedient. Can he understand what you just said?"

"Yeah, he can't talk, but he can understand you just fine. I think he'll be much better to train and take care of than a regular horse. Wanna try riding him?" Even though there wasn't a harness attached to John's back, Nikola boldly straddled him. In response, the creature began to walk around.

At Nikola's command, John picked up his pace. The walk slowly developed into a small trot, and then a fully-fledged run. Before long, John fluttered out his wings and leaped high into the air. After flying for a small bit, not too high mind you, John landed back on the ground with an amazed Nikola in tow.

"Well, how was it?"

"It… It was incredible. The height is certainly something I'll have to get used to, but I'm certain I'll conquer such things in time." As he spoke, he had John fly upward again. Nikola looked extremely happy with himself. I didn't have a rope or anything to moor them in, so I was a bit worried about them floating away…

"Milord! What about me?! I'd like one too!" Norn suddenly shuffled closer to me. I was surprised an unruly girl like her had taken to calling me something so polite, but it seemed that was just how it was in this world. Lain, though a bit more subdued, was also exhibiting a similar look of excitement.

Sheesh, I was gonna summon something even without you guys getting all excited about it. Hmph… it'd be boring if I just called in another Griffin, though… These two are girls, so I know exactly what they'd like!

"Come forth, Dark! I seek a skyhorse, [Pegasus]!" After the fog cleared and the magic circle disappeared, two pure-white horses with magnificent wings appeared from nothing.

"Whoa! Amazing! They're so pretty!" Norn ran up to one of them and started brushing its back. Lain, ever-reserved, timidly touched one of their wings.

"Ah, these two are called Anne and Diana. Anne, you pair up with Norn, and Diana can go with Lain." The Pegasi wiggled their heads in affirmation. Anne lowered her head immediately and prompted Norn to get on. Just like Nikola, Norn straddled the horse and slowly warmed up by trotting around. After a short amount of time, they leaped high into the air.

After a few moments of apprehension, Lain climbed up onto Diana and flew high up into the sky.

The three of them finally landed after circling the castle a few times. I ignored their overexcited actions and took some of the harvested monster leather from [Storage]. I used that to make saddles, stirrups, reins, and so on. Then, I handed them over to the three of them.

I told them to spend some time flying overhead and checking on the territory of the country itself. They'd be able to practice controlling their mounts at the same time, so it would all work out quite nicely. I told them not to worry if trouble occurred, because the summoned beasts could telepathically link to me and alert me of any danger.

I said they could have the afternoon off, but Nikola seemed to readily accept his job and wanted to spend the whole day scouting the region out. That guy was stoic and extremely dutiful.

As for myself, there were things I had to do that didn't involve my soldiers. On the first floor of my castle, I redesigned the interior of a small room. It now had a huge mirror on the wall, big enough for a person to pass through. I also installed a metal plate nearby.

"Touya, bruv. Wot's all this, then?"

"If you touch the metal plate, a [Gate] should open, and it'll record who the last person to go through was. Only authorized personnel can use this, too. It's a way of verifying your identity." Renne was staring at the mirror, eyes wide with wonder, so I gave her a little explanation. There weren't any touch sensors in this world, and it wouldn't really work if I enchanted it with [Search] or something similar. If someone decided to use transformation magic to disguise themselves, then it was possible that they'd be able to pass through without any issue. In the end, I decided to apply a [Program] to an iron plate that scanned the fingerprints and magical wavelengths of people that touched it.

"On top of that, you can set the destination. But right now we only have Belfast." I had set up similar mirrors back at my Belfast home.

Should I buy small properties in Mismede and Regulus, maybe? Nah, better to wait until the kings grant me formal embassies there

13

or something… Hm… I think it'd be fine with the emperor of Regulus, but the beastking doesn't really know about my [Gate] *spell… Well, I'll work that out later.*

"So, Renne. Wanna help me test it? Touch that metal plate."

"Like this?" Renne did as she was told and raised a hand up to the plate. I think I might've placed it a little too high. The moment Renne touched the metal plate, it let off a shimmer and her name appeared on it.

In turn, the mirror began to shimmer and shine as the [Gate] warmed up.

"Alright, and where do you wanna go?"

"Huh? Uh… the mansion at Belfast!" The mirror let out an even more dazzling sparkle in response to Renne's words. Renne then walked into it and vanished from the room. *Great, guess it works.*

I touched the metal plate and quickly followed after her. I set it so only the last person to touch the metal plate could pass through the portal, which meant that people would need to touch the plate one by one as they passed through. It was just a security measure. That way bad guys couldn't pass through after us or anything, either.

After I passed through the mirror, I came out in the Belfast mansion. The first thing I noticed was that Renne wasn't there.

I opened the door and went out into the hall, then I faintly heard Renne's voice coming from the home's main entrance. I wondered if we had a guest or something.

"Something up, Renne?"

"Oh uh, bruv— Er, sir… A letter's gone and come from the royal palace."

Tom, our gatekeeper, was at the entrance. He handed the letter over. Tom and the others manning this place were currently living in the old area that Julio and Crea lived in before they moved to the castle.

I looked over the letter, and it said I was needed immediately at Belfast's royal court. I wondered what they wanted.

"Oh goodness gracious me... You must be the young man everyone's abuzz about, Mochizuki Touya! Or, er, Grand Duke, I suppose!"

"Yeah..." His Majesty the King of Belfast introduced me to a bald-headed man. He kind of looked similar to that one Hollywood actor who played the world's unluckiest detective. More importantly, this baldy was actually Rig Reek Refreese, the emperor of the Refreese Imperium. Of course, that also made him the father of that annoying author. You know, the one who wrote *those* things.

"The king of Belfast has told me of your exploits. I can't possibly believe that you quelled an entire coup alone."

"Ah, well, I mean, it's not like I..." I didn't know why, but I suddenly came off as a little defensive and apologetic. In response to that, Refreese's emperor simply grinned.

"...I see, then. It is as the good king said! You don't seem to have any impure aims."

"Sorry, but, uh... I don't quite know what you mean."

"You are a man who singlehandedly took down a trained army and a legion of monsters, and you're also engaged to marry princesses from both Regulus and Belfast. From the perspective of my nation, you're a considerable threat."

Ah... I guess I didn't consider how it might look to an outsider. That was probably inevitable though, despite my intentions.

"I'm not sure about the situations of the other countries, but they're probably keeping their heads down for the time being. They

15

may end up fearing that if they anger you, you could come and collapse their governments."

"I don't plan on getting involved in politics like that, though." *Well, that's only true to a certain extent. If a country dispatched an assassin and killed Yumina for political gain or something, I'm not sure if I could forgive that… I'd definitely drag the mastermind behind something like that out and hurt him so bad he'd wish I'd killed him. But for the most part, I definitely have no plans to do anything right now. That doesn't necessarily mean anyone will believe that, though.*

"We at the Refreese Imperium would like to deepen our relationship with you, Grand Duke. Normally, we would ask for you to take my daughter as your bride…"

"No, that's not necessary! No, really, honestly. No thank you!" *I do not want that woman near me. I seriously don't.*

"Fret not, I'm saying that we would ask, had I not already promised her to another foreign kingdom. I'm afraid I can't rescind that engagement, it's quite a shame."

More like a stroke of luck. I already feel bad for her husband-to-be. I hope he'll be alright. Come to think of it, her novel-writing is a secret even to her father, right? Guess she'll keep it under wraps with the hubby, too.

"At any rate, I'll get to my point. Your castle was recently completed in Brunhild, was it not? If so, I'd request an audience with you there. A friendly gathering, of kings and emperors. What say you? No political agenda, simply a night of merrymaking."

"So wait, you want me to invite over the rulers of the western states or something?" *Does he mean just himself, or everyone…?* As I mulled the proposition over, the king of Belfast turned to me with a smile.

"Hmhm... Belfast, Refreese, Mismede, Regulus... I think all four leaders of these nations should converge upon Brunhild for a night of festivities."

"...You want to do this?"

Both men suddenly spoke up in unison.

"Even a ruler needs time off now and then!"

Oh dear.

"Every so often we need time to relax, play, and forget our royal positions. I'm sure you can prepare something to help ease our weary minds, my boy."

Well, it was true that I came from a country that specialized in entertainment, and this world didn't really have much to compare it to, but... Wasn't inviting every one of these rulers a pretty big deal? I'd have to go all-out on the food, the entertainment, and the defenses.

"Don't overthink it, understand? Simply invite us as you would invite a regular set of friends." The emperor spoke up, but it didn't really change the complexity of the situation.

What kind of implications will this have, anyway? It'd be good to improve my standing with the other nations, but still... I could just deny them, but why do they have to glare at me with puppy-dog eyes?! I guess you just went and decided without me, huh?

"Very well, then. I'll invite you all formally. But please, no politics in my home. No in-fighting, or agreement drafting."

"We understand. Might we bring our families as well?"

"That's reasonable, but please only bring five people per monarch, yourselves included. I don't have a lot of staff in the castle just yet."

Ugh, I can see this going poorly... I hope their whole families don't show up. Looks like things are gonna get real busy real fast...

Alrighty then... Inviting them was one thing, but working on entertainment was another. They said they wanted to relax and play, so I started there. I decided to create something within the realm of reason and simplicity.

The first thing I created was a pool table. That game was simple enough to enjoy both indoors and outdoors.

Next up came the installation of a bowling alley. I set up a basic **[Program]** to return the bowling ball and pick the pins back up, so it wasn't especially difficult to automate. After I made it, I considered that it might be a little too intense for the kings. They were getting on in age, after all.

Next, I created an automated mahjong deck. It would definitely take them a long time to memorize the rules properly, but I had a feeling they'd come to enjoy it if they got used to it.

And then, I created a bunch of classic indoor entertainment games like pinball, air hockey, and table tennis. I also made a bunch of automated massage chairs so they could relieve some tension.

I made this myself, but... I totally deserve a go, right? A-Ahh... it's so good... I'm soothed already. Guess I was more worn out than I thought...

"Touya, Touya!"

"Hm?" I was suddenly called from my euphoric daydream by Elze, who was seated at the mahjong table. She was pointing at the tiles in front of her.

"This one's a win, right?"

"Let me see here... Wait, what?!" *Dai suuishi, Tsuiisou, Suuankou, and a single wait...*

"So that's a win by drawing? A tsumo, was it?"

"Yep, that's a tsumo. That's a triple, no a quintuple yakuman. And since you're the dealer that's eighty thousand points from everyone."

"WHAT?!" Lapis, Cecilia, and Linze, who were playing against Elze, all threw up their arms in despair.

How horrifying... I made a mental note to never play with Elze.

"Hey, boss... Between a flush and a straight, which is better?"

"Uhh... a flush, I'm pretty sure." Sylvie and Belle were both sitting at the poker table, learning the rules.

I had the girls from Moon Reader come over to help with tending to the guests, since the castle was short staffed. Sylvie, Belle, and Shea all came over to help out. Sylvie was the head waitress, Belle manned the reception desk, and Shea was a real wiz in the kitchen, so we covered all our bases.

I had Sylvie and the others play the games with the maids from our home, since I figured it was the fastest way for them to get a grasp on the rules.

"Siiir, please remove Cesca from the poool table. She won't let me have the cueeee."

"Silence! I'm calculating the angle of reflection, the incidence level, and meting out how much force I should apply. As I work those out, it should be a paltry task to win!" Cecile spoke up in a concerned tone, but Cesca simply replied to her matter-of-factly.

I might've sent her to the wrong game... If she keeps pocketing balls without missing, then it'll become a break and run out situation, and Cecile will never get a go...

I left the game room for a bit and went to the dining room and kitchen. Crea and Shea were both working hard, while Renne was offering them assistance.

"Ah, good sir. Your timing is perfect as ever, please give this a try." Crea passed me a freshly baked and piping hot dessert, so I bit into it. *Ooh, that's good!*

"Ah, I'm glad that you figured out how to make a good waffle. It tastes really good. If you put whipped cream on it, you can make it even tastier, though."

"I see… We'll try and make that as well, then!" I held the waffle in my mouth, made my way over to the fridge, and leaned down and took something out. *Good, it solidified well.*

"What's that, boss?" Shea tilted her head and expressed confusion at the item.

"It's pudding. It's another item you can add cream and fruits to. Tastes really good." It'd be more accurate to call it 'pudding a la mode' if it had the stuff on it, though. I took out a plate and turned the pudding upside down, letting it slide out on to the surface.

The yellow caramel oozed out slowly, making my mouth water a bit. I grabbed a spoon and took a scoop of the tasty mass I'd created. *Hm, a little thick, but it's still yummy!*

Shea took a spoon and put a scoop of her own into her mouth. She opened her eyes in amazement and her mouth flapped a little like a fish. *Guess she likes it.*

"Hey bruv, I cut the potatoes like you asked, but what am I supposed to do now?" There was a pile of neatly-cut potato sticks on the chopping board in front of Renne. I went over and washed them a bit in the sink, then added some oil to a frying pan. Then, I set the heat to medium and began to drop the potato sticks in one by one.

Once they started to float, I took them out. After that, I upped the heat and deep fried them until they were a crispy brown.

I sprinkled some fresh salt on to them and garnished them with a side of homemade ketchup. After going so long without french fries I felt an unreasonable amount of joy toward something so mundane.

"These are bloody amazing, bruv! Can I have them all?!"

"…All of them? Well, you can take them all, but I wouldn't recommend stuffing your face with them, you'll get an upset tummy." I gave Renne a soft smile and passed the french fries over to her. She wolfed down a handful before I could even react. Crea and Shea peeked their heads over and grabbed a bunch all of a sudden, chowing down like it was some kind of ambrosia. …*They're gonna get fat. Oh geez.*

With that, the indoor entertainment and the food were on track. Now all I had to check on was the defense system.

As I went out into the training grounds, I noticed my three soldiers sprawled out on the ground, panting heavily. Yae was laughing softly at them, for whatever reason.

Still, it wasn't she who had driven them to this state, it was the grizzled old mustache-clad man, as well as the scarred beast of a man who were standing next to her.

Baba and Yamagata, two famed commanders from the Takeda-controlled territory of Eashen. They were two of the Takeda Elite Four, renowned for their martial prowess.

"Hey, squirt. Somethin' up?"

"No, just coming by to see how things are going." As usual, old man Baba decided to call me something annoying. *Aren't I the ruler of a country now?! Damn it…*

"Hey, Touya. These three show great potential. They need a little polish, but I am quite sure they can shine brightly." Yamagata grinned at me, his broadsword resting on his shoulders. *And this guy's just casually calling me Touya. I see how it is.*

I had specifically called upon those two to train my three knights. I briefly considered asking Neil or Yae's older brother, but the two of them seemed busy, so I opted not to. These two, on the other hand, had nothing but free time, apparently.

From what I had heard, Takeda's son succeeded the clan and immediately pushed away all the close advisers that had ties to his father. He then embarked on a strange, selfish campaign where he just did whatever he wanted. Despite my advice, they had gotten into a quarrel with Oda as well for whatever reason.

I wondered if it was his young age that made him reckless, or if he was simply an incompetent person. It was possible that the downfall of Takeda was simply something that happened in many worlds...

"But still, a brat like you governing an entire country? Even if it's small, that's still somethin' special. Well, I guess I've seen the magic you can come up with, so it's not too surprisin', but still..."

"Yes, I'm rather amazed and a little envious. When you compare Touya to our young lord... Hmph..." Yamagata sighed a bit wistfully and muttered as he looked at the exhausted trio. Seemed like they had a lot to worry about.

"So what's the situation now? Is Oda being aggressive or what?"

"Nay, in this case the problems don't stem from Oda, but our lord himself. He gives orders on a whim without considering the implications, and when the money coffers run low he simply raises the taxes. To be frank, he is not popular with the people at all. Rather than us destroying Oda with ease, it may be them that swoop in and wipe us out. With how things are going, we're considerably weakened. We Elite Four have tried to advise him, but he bullheadedly ignores all we have to offer." Sounded to me like things had gone from bad to terrible. Even if the founder of a nation was a tactical genius or a benevolent man, it wouldn't be the first time a country has been driven to ruin by the foolish attitude of the next generation. Schingen probably wouldn't be able to rest in peace, after all.

"If you'd like, you're welcome to defect to my country. We're just starting out, so we could really use the extra hands."

"Hmph… I'll admit, squirt… that's quite the encitin' offer ya got there. But we still got plenty obligations to Lord Takeda, so…"

"Come, Baba-dono, aren't you being a little stiff? We've been invited here out of the kindness of the boy's heart. I'd be quite happy to join this place, but the lack of an ongoing war is a little saddening."

That was a dangerous thing you just said! Battle nuts like him were a real problem, though he'd probably get along with Mismede's Beastking.

"Whatever our feelings are on the matter right now, we cannot give you an answer. We'd need to return home and discuss the issue with the other two. Even if Takeda is brought to ruin, I feel we should look upon it with our own eyes."

"I understand, so don't worry. I won't press the issue for the time being."

"That's most appreciated." Yamagata lowered his sword and shifted his attention to the three who were still on the ground.

"Alright, you little mites! Same as last time, I'll charge the three of you at once!"

"Yes sir!" The three of them drew their weapons with renewed vigor as they let out that cry. Their fighting spirit was pretty impressive, but I wondered if it was enough to defend against his onslaught. Regardless of the outcome, it was something they had to do alone.

I turned back to the castle after checking out the training grounds, and the big double doors opened for me as I approached. Then, as I stepped into the entrance hall, they closed again. They weren't automatic doors or anything. The person who had opened them was right in front of me. Or rather, hanging up in front of me.

It was a picture hanging up in the middle of the landing on the stairs just in front of me.

《The caaastle is raaaather lively today, Master.》A girl in a white dress protruded her upper body out of the picture frame and made a casual comment. It was the picture frame artifact I had recovered during the ghost fiasco. When she realized that I was the man who controlled Babylon, she copied Cesca and started to call me master.

I sold the picture of the dead feudal lord's wife a while ago, and placed a different picture in the frame using the proceeds. It was a nice picture, so I decided to decorate my castle with it.

As a result, she was reborn as a girl in her late teens, clad in a beautiful white dress and a pink ribbon in her hair. She called herself Ripple. Apparently the castle she inhabited beforehand was called Ripple Castle, so that was probably why.

"Everyone's busy preparing to host the other countries' leaders. You gonna help too, Ripple?"

《Yes! I'll keep on the lookouuut for anything suspicious. My eyes are everywhere in this place, after all. Ahaaa, young Renne just smashed a plaate!》I didn't understand it too well myself, but Ripple managed to reproduce her frame using the workshop, and was now capable of moving around through the frames as she pleased. Apparently they couldn't copy her soul, so there was still only one Ripple. She was basically a security camera network at this point.

I put pictures of landscapes and scenery in the new frames and placed them all over the castle. I took care not to put any in the private quarters, however. I guess she could be called a ghostly surveillance camera.

With that, I figured everything was in order. All that was left was to greet the incoming royals.

"Ohoho! Amazing, I don't know what it is, but it's amazing!" The second he walked into the game room, the king of Belfast turned toward the pinball machine with a look of glee on his face. Following after him, but turning in the complete opposite direction, the beastking walked over to the bowling alley.

"Aha, there's some weight to this, boy! A cannonball, perhaps? No, it has three holes…" Entering after those two, the two emperors looked around the room with cautious eyes.

"Is all of this for playing around? It isn't especially gaudy here." The emperor of Regulus murmured a bit, and from behind him came all the family members that the monarchs had brought with them.

Initially I had told them to only bring close family, but apparently their governmental members were concerned so they brought a small retinue of guardsmen as well.

From Belfast there was His Majesty the King, Queen Yuel, Duke Ortlinde, Duchess Ellen, and Sue.

From Regulus there was His Highness the Emperor, Crown Prince Lux, and Princess Sarah.

From Refreese, His Imperial Presence the Emperor, Empress Zelda, Princess Reliel, and Crown Prince Redis.

From Mismede, there was His Beastliness the Beastking, Queen Thillie, First Prince Remza, Second Prince Alba, and First Princess Thea.

There were seventeen people in total. They also each had a small entourage of armed guards.

From Belfast there was Neil and Lyon. From Regulus there was Commander Gaspar. From Mismede, there was Garm. And the guards from Refreese I knew nothing about at all. Around five people came from each country, so the count was closer to twenty guests in the end. Their weapons were confiscated in case of any shenanigans, and I had applied a [Paralyze] effect that would take hold if anything funny went down.

The guardsmen, upon seeing the room and its wonders for the first time, seemed quite taken aback. Our three soldiers were situated in the game room just in case anything happened. They looked extremely nervous, though… Still, that was only natural. The defense of the castle itself was being left to a Cerberus, a Griffin, and two Pegasi, so the exterior would be mostly fine.

"Welcome, dear guests, to our game room. The various devices and creations here are assembled for you all to use at your own leisure. If you wish to know how they function, simply ask a member of our household and we will be happy to assist." Elze, Linze, Yae, Yumina, Lu, and the maids were all lined up for our guests. Lapis, Cecile, Renne, Cesca, and the girls from Moon Reader were here to assist as well. Rosetta had even taken a rare change of pace and gotten into a maid outfit rather than her regular overalls. And of course, supervising all of them was my esteemed and magnificent butler, Laim.

"Hot food, desserts, drinks and so forth are just over there. Feel free to eat at your own discretion." I had prepared various tables and chairs, as well as the luxurious massage chairs, in the corner of the game room. On the tables were various samples of fine food.

Each of the rulers wandered off toward the games, their eyes full of curiosity and wonder. On the other hand, their wives and children seemed more interested in the various pieces of confectionery tucked away in the corner of the room.

"Haaah!" Without further ado, the beastking beelined straight for the bowling ball and gave it a firm toss. Despite his furious yelling, it was a gutterball. Prince Remza and Prince Alba did the same thing, too. Remza looked to be about nine, while Alba seemed to be about five. They both were snow leopard beastmen, like their father.

At the air hockey table, Duke Ortlinde and His Majesty the King were engaged in a high-stakes confrontation between brothers.

At the mahjong table, a showdown was ongoing between His Imperial Presence the Emperor and his son, Crown Prince Redis.

Crown Prince Redis was twelve years old, if I recalled correctly. He seemed extremely mature, but being the younger brother of *that* girl must've been extremely unpleasant. Just as I had thought during the coup incident, Prince Lux didn't have much of a presence to him. I couldn't believe this guy was going to get married and succeed his father. It was pretty surprising, really.

Lapis answered any and all questions about mahjong with relative ease. People picked up on it pretty easily because I had put up a visual aid for scoring combos next to the board.

It looked like the guards were enjoying themselves watching the games unfold, too.

At the dining table, the food was proving especially popular with the women. I was pretty pleased to see them all getting along.

Sue, Reliel, Thea, and Renne were at the cards table, playing what appeared to be Old Maid. Princess Thea seemed to be about the same age as Sue, ten or so.

"This is something amazing, isn't it…" Neil stood nearby, muttering something. The one to respond to him was Gaspar.

"Quite so. Never thought I'd see the day that all the rulers of the western continent would band together like this. It's rather relieving to see them let loose and have some fun." Both of them smiled as they played pool and looked over their respective charges.

The rulers didn't seem to mind who won or lost the games, so they were just going at all the ones they could fit in at a time.

"Touya, what's this one?" The beastking turned to me and pointed at a small stand with six holes in it. He picked up the soft foam hammer attached to the side, then peeked into one of the holes.

Seeing him reminded me that my ability to use [Gate] was revealed to Mismede not too long ago. They doubted it at first, apparently, but Leen vouching for me was enough for them to believe it in the end. It didn't matter too much at this point, since the Regulus Empire was also aware of what I could do.

The beastking didn't really seem to care anyway. I decided to teach him how whack-a-mole worked.

"So, in this game you have to score points by smacking the little moles that pop out of the holes. It'd be best if you didn't strike using full force, since even a little impact should register." Yep, the game was whack-a-mole. The moment the game started, the beastking immediately struck the moles with astonishing precision. Just as one would expect of a species predisposed to war… his senses were sharp. *But you're naive, Beastking!*

"I-It can't be!" Halfway through the game, the moles picked up the pace and jumped up and down several times in quick succession. In the end, His Beastliness ended the game with ninety-two points.

"Ghaugh! One more time, I'll defeat you!" Despite the fact that I told him not to smack them too hard, he went at it full-force. I had expected something like this, however, so I made sure to build an extremely sturdy frame for this particular game.

I looked back toward the dining table and found that the women were all giggling, chatting, and picking at various desserts. That was good. Cecile and Laim had the situation under control over there, so I turned my attention back to the games.

"Excuse me, Grand Duke? How do you play with this thing, sir?" The two young princes of Mismede approached me, asking about a certain thing I had placed in the corner of the room. It was a cube-shaped trampoline enclosure with transparent sides. Through magic means, you could jump around and bounce off all six sides.

"You go in through the entrance and can jump around inside. It should support up to two adults at a time, so you two will be just fine. Give it a go." The two snow leopard boys bounded into the entrance and began to jump around. It didn't take long for them to let loose entirely. After a while they began to do backflips and crazy parkour stuff. Beastmen truly were astonishingly talented…

"Oho, that seems rather fun. Perhaps a tad intense for me…" His Highness the Emperor watched the boys playing and laughed gently.

"I've placed some special chairs over here to relieve tension. It might feel a little strange at first, but I assure you it'll have you feeling comfy and refreshed in no time."

"Oho?" I guided the old emperor over to the massage chairs and helped him sit down on it. After that, I let the magic flow through it. The rollers in the back of the chair and the pumps around the legs and bottom of the chair began to function, slowly beginning a full-body massage. The emperor frowned a little at first, but he was smiling gently with his eyes closed before long.

"Ohooo… i-it's so nice… It feels amazing… Th-Thank you…"

"If you want it to stop, just press this button."

"Mm… yes…" Regardless of whether or not he heard me, I moved off away from the emperor to let him enjoy his relaxation time.

A short bit away, His Imperial Presence the Emperor of Refreese and the beastking were having a bout of mini golf. Across from them, Prince Lux was playing table tennis with Duke Ortlinde. And a bit away from those guys, His Majesty the King of Belfast was playing pool with Gaspar. *Wait, is it fine for the guardsmen to be playing too?!*

"The king invited him, and the emperor permitted it. Sure must be nice to be Gaspar right now… I wish I could play too." Lyon walked up to me and let out a small lament. He had a small point, but I imagine you probably weren't allowed to win if you were playing against the king of another country. I guess it could count as work, too… entertaining the king with pool and all.

"Feel free to come here when you have a day off. We can play. Oh, actually. When you get married to Olga, you could come celebrate here."

"Seriously?! That would be incredible! My fellow knights will be delighted!" I wondered if I should invite all the knights… I figured I should, it seemed standard fare. Everyone who knew them would be gathered here to have some fun. It'd be like the wedding dinner, really, just with more of a relaxed, party-style atmosphere.

After playing for a time, the men diverted their attention to the food and drink on display, which meant that the women were now more than ready to give the games a go. That being said, they didn't opt for the physically exerting activities like trampolining or bowling. Instead, they decided to play cards, mahjong, pinball, and other lighter activities.

"Now then, if you would allow the nobility of the Duchy of Brunhild to grant you all a modest gift, please step this way." Things were quieting down as the attendees ran out of games to play, so I called out to them. The maids then began to distribute small cards to everyone in the room. Each card had twenty-five random numbers written on them in a grid. I then directed everyone's attention to a lottery machine, and told them to mark down on their cards the number that came out. To be blunt, we were playing bingo.

I removed a cloth sheet from a pile in the corner of the room to unveil the prizes.

There was a wide variety of goods on display, from weaponry to house decorations and ornaments. There were even some spellstone-imbued accessories for the ladies. Stuffed toys for the kids, too. The weapons were no mere lumps of material I had crafted, either. Each had a unique enchantment applied to it. That being said, I made sure the weapons weren't especially overpowered or anything, just unique in their functions.

"Alrighty, let's start with… Eight! The first number is eight! Mark on your cards where the number eight is, if it's there at all. After you get a set of numbers, or a bingo, in a horizontal, diagonal, or vertical line, you win a prize!" In this instance, I had actually prepared enough gifts for everyone to get one. It was more about who won first.

After a few matches, there seemed to be some people close to winning prizes.

"Two… two… I need a two!"

"Come on, fourteen!"

"Fifty-oneeee, pleaaaase." Everyone stared in anticipation as the machine whirred and clicked.

"Thirty-two! We got thirty-two!"

"Bingo!" The one to shout out was Gaspar, Commander of the Regulus Empire's knights. After I checked his card, I showed him to the prizes.

"So, which one are you going for?"

"You mean to say I can choose from any of these?"

"That's right, but you can only have one." Gaspar chose his gift after some deliberation. He opted for the ornate red lance.

"I call this the Blaster Lance. If you recite a certain phrase, it'll shoot a potent blast of fire from the tip."

"What, really?!"

"Yeah, I'll teach you the phrase later on. It'd be bad if you fired it here." I chuckled a bit at my own joke and handed the lance to Gaspar. He happily held it in hand for a bit before returning to where he was before.

He showed it off to the emperor, who seemed quite keenly interested in how it worked. The man looked at it with a mixture of amazement and admiration, so I wasn't quite sure what he was thinking.

It consumed a lot of mana, so an ordinary person would be fit to collapse after firing it off just three times. That was why I had designed this weapon as a special trump card, only to be used properly.

"Alright folks, let's see what we've got next! Number... fifteen! Fifteen, folks!" The bingo game progressed without a hitch, and everyone was happy with their prizes. The ruler's wives were especially happy with the accessories and interior decoration-related rewards they had chosen. Young Princess Thea of Mismede received a plush toy, as well. I had given it a [**Program**] that caused it to repeat anything that was said to it. It was just a shame that it happened to be voiced by that irritating robogirl.

"Now, it's quite late and night has fallen. If you'd all please follow me for the last of today's events." I took everyone along with me to the castle balcony. The sky was black as pitch, and the moon was nowhere to be seen. There was nothing besides the castle in the area either, so the landscape was also as dark as could be.

Suddenly, an enormous blast occurred in the sky, sending out a colored flower spreading far across the sky. The guardsmen put themselves into defensive positions, but I raised my hand to put them at ease.

"Ah, these are fireworks. You simply sit back and appreciate them, you do. They are often launched during the summer in Eashen, they are." Yae had confirmed to me that fireworks existed in Eashen, but it seemed like they didn't have anything especially flashy, just basic rockets.

The fireworks bloomed out into the night sky, one after the other. To be honest, I didn't actually fire them upward. I had Rosetta drop them from the Workshop of Babylon, which was hidden in stealth mode. I had written a [**Program**] to ensure that the fireworks would detonate before hitting the ground. It was much easier than creating pyrotechnic launchers.

From the balcony, we stood and watched beautiful flowers bloom in the air. Our maids passed out champagne to all the adults who were staring up at the display. The kids were extremely excited too, looking up to the firework with wonder in their eyes.

With that, the Duchy of Brunhild's founding party came to a close. It was a huge success.

In the end, after I told each of the monarchs that they could take one thing from my game room back home with them, each of them chose to take a massage chair. Leading a nation must have been tiresome work after all...

The founding party went off without a hitch, and soon a sense of peace began to fall over Brunhild.

Despite the fact that it had taken a short while due to various issues, I finally gave Lu an engagement ring. I definitely couldn't have afforded to put it off any longer. Not to mention that it would've been extremely rude not to formally put a ring on her.

Even though she acted as though she didn't mind the delay, Lu gratefully and happily accepted what I gave her. The ring was identical to the ones I had given to the others, right down to the design and magical effects.

"Now I can finally hold my head high and proclaim that I am the fiancee of Touya, my amazing man!" I felt a pang of guilt wash over me as I looked at her smiling. I definitely shouldn't have put it off so long.

We were all happily sitting together at a table on the balcony when Leen appeared with Paula in tow. Her expression was grave.

"There's been another Phrase sighting. One has appeared within the Sea of Trees. The tribe living there sent a request for help to Mismede." Everyone suddenly jumped up from their seats in a panic. Except Lu, who had no idea what any of that meant.

"And what became of it? Was it taken down?" Yumina asked.

"I'm afraid not. It's still there right now, demolishing the tribal village, and turning any and all individuals that enter the vicinity into mincemeat. From what I understand, it has a huge, arachnid form."

*A gigantic Spider Phrase? I wonder if it's on the same tier as the Manta Phrase we encountered a while back... What if it's even stronger? If that's the case, then [**Apport**] won't do the trick... I'd like to try and smash it using [**Gravity**], though.*

"Let's go, then. I don't know if we can take it down, but we have to at least try. Not just that, we might—"

"If we're lucky, we may encounter that boy again." I nodded at Leen's comment. It was like she had read my mind.

Ende. The mysterious young man who had so easily crushed the Manta Phrase that we stood no chance against. I wanted to know what he meant when he spoke of the "Sovereign Phrase." That guy knew something, he had to.

"Let's get to Babylon and set course for the Sea of Trees." We began our preparations to face off against this new Phrase.

"Crystal creatures that destroyed the civilizations of old?" We were traveling along to the Sea of Trees in our Babylon, so we decided to roughly explain the situation to Lu while we had the chance.

Come to think of it, what even are the Phrase? Right now I'm just assuming that they were sealed in some area of space, and those tears in reality are where they're slipping through as the barrier that's keeping them contained breaks down. So now they're finally returning to the world after thousands of years... Probably, I think. If I believe what Ende had to say, then the creatures are searching for their leader, the Sovereign Phrase. But from where I'm looking all they've been doing is killing everything in their vicinity. Is there more to it, or is it just mindless slaughter? Wait, what even happened all those years ago? Who sealed them in the first place, if they are actually sealed.

Where did the Phrase come from? I don't have any answers at all here! Ende... he probably knows. He warped off last time without so much as an explanation, but I'll make him talk if he shows up again...

"Master, we've reached our destination." Cesca called to me and displayed a scene from below on the monolith computer. An enormous beast of crystal was rampaging around the forest. It was an arachnid monster with eight thin, sharp legs. Those legs were cutting through trees like they were butter, skewering members of a tribal village who happened to live down there all the while.

"It's a big one. About the same size as the last one we encountered," I said.

"Verily, it is. I am just thankful that this one does not appear to have the power of flight, I am." I was just as thankful as Yae. Fighting the Manta Phrase was a huge chore because it was soaring above the desert sands. The forest was less open, so we had more blind spots to hide in. We just had to make sure none of those giant trees crushed us or whatever.

"We need to hurry, now. The village will be completely lost if we don't take action." As we made preparations to reach the surface, we saw the tribeswomen firing arrows and invoking magic against the Spider Phrase.

However, it shrugged off their attacks like they were nothing. As it roared, the creature absorbed all magic in the vicinity, including all of the spells that touched it. It seemed to work in a different way to the Drainbracer, and it wasn't a nullifying effect like the Demon Lord's, but either way it was a dangerous power that converted magical energy used against it into more fuel.

The tanned tribal women brandished curved swords and tried facing it once more, but the Phrase simply swung out one of its sharp limbs and gutted them.

37

"Itsh! Miyohmanah, Tacohdeejeekah! Garinoh!" One young tribal girl barked out what seemed to be orders, but I couldn't understand what she was saying. It was odd to me that I didn't understand her, as I had kind of just assumed God had given me an omnilingual body or something.

At any rate, she looked to be their leader. At her command, the bow-wielding girls retreated immediately. It looked like they were trying to create a flanking formation in order to let the non-combatants retreat.

One of the enormous creature's legs suddenly raised in the air, then went bolting toward the shouting woman like a thrown spear.

"[Accel Boost]!" I sped through the trees like a madman, taking the mithril greatsword out of [Storage] as I charged. Just in time to stop her from being impaled, I intercepted the creature's leg and deflected it away from the girl. In a flash, I grabbed her and took her into my arms. Her eyes went wide with surprise as I leaped backward, putting a great deal of distance between us and the Spider Phrase.

I set her down, brandishing my blade once more.

"Get to safety, focus on evacuating, and… you have no idea what I'm saying, do you?" I tried to point to her, and then the deeper forest in an attempt to explain through signing. She either didn't get it or ignored me, choosing to walk up to me instead.

"Emoh. Ortettkoeecheeh. Merkoh! Sahnatoanehko! Boko boko!"

"N-No, I can't understand you…" I finally took a moment to get a good look at the girl, and realized she was very much the image of a warrior. She brandished an axe in one hand, and was decorated with red war paint all over her body.

She had healthy-looking tanned brown skin, but I was a little unnerved by how little she was wearing. Only a single scrap of fabric bound her chest, and her lower body was covered by a crudely-constructed loincloth. She had sandal-like shoes and improved wraps on her hands, but she was practically fighting half-naked! Something gave me the impression that these tribes lived a very different life to those in the major cities.

This girl's gotta be around the same age as me, but she's packing some incredible assets... They're practically heaving and asking to be freed from behind that chest binding she's wearing! I quickly realized I was staring a little too south, then immediately rectified the situation.

"Emohoomaynaggredo! Ohcheenakuhoho! Kakanoha! Kellesohrise!" She was ranting and raving about something or other, but I couldn't tell what she meant. I wondered if she was mad at me for staring.

I pushed such thoughts out of my mind and took my sword into my hand. It was time to face down the enemy. I aimed for one of its legs... And, at the moment my blade angled down toward it, I activated [**Gravity**]. The thin leg was reduced to mere fragments beneath the super-bolstered weight of my greatsword.

"Amazing, it actually worked!" Unfortunately, the shattered leg regenerated within seconds. The creature had absorbed all of the magic the people used against it some time ago. Just as I'd figured, the only way to take this thing out would be to destroy the core.

There were three cores on its head, all lined up in a row. They glowed a faint orange, much like the Manta Phrase cores had in my last encounter.

"Linze, Leen! Give him the old ice one-two!" As I yelled, the two of them began the incantation to cast [**Ice Rock**], and a massive chunk landed on the spider from above. The Spider Phrase dipped its body for a brief moment, but began to resist the weight, pushing upward with a loud straining sound. *Sorry pal, but I can't let you do that.*

I jumped up to the ice block bearing down on it, then activated [Gravity] to increase the block's weight tenfold.

A slow creaking echoed out as the Spider Phrase strained, and then I heard a new noise. The sound of shattering ice. The enormous rock was unable to support its own weight and began to splinter. Frankly, I was surprised it had held it together for so long to begin with.

The ice buckled, raining down in thin sheets. The Spider Phrase, released from the crushing force, leaped high up in the air. Timing my strike as I fell down toward it, I activated [Gravity] on my greatsword and swung it down at the creature.

"Shatter to pieces, you bastard!" I struck the Spider Phrase with such a force that the ground began to quake.

A shattering sound echoed out as the monster split into thousands of pieces, and yet it was still standing. Regardless of that, I had shattered the head, exposing the cores amongst the ruined fragments. Using Brunhild, I took them out in quick succession.

"Guh…" Somehow, I had done it. It was much easier than the last time, as well. But I guess I had [Gravity] to thank for that. It would've been better if I used the spell on the Phrase directly, but beggars couldn't be choosers. I looked at my greatsword, noticing that the mithril blade had been bent out of shape.

"Emoh… Nonamehotoh?" The brown-skinned girl muttered something, staring in abject amazement. I had no idea what she was saying, but her expressions spoke wonders for her surprise.

I looked around to check on the injured, finding myself staring at a field of fallen people. The situation was bad.

"Target Lock. Target any injured person within a radius of five hundred meters. Invoke [Cure Heal]."

"Understood. Targets acquired. Invoking [**Cure Heal**]." The voice buzzed out of my smartphone as a magical light enveloped the wounded, gently tending to their injuries. Those who had visible injuries quickly found themselves with no open wounds to speak of.

The young girl, upon seeing my sorcery, ran toward her collapsed allies.

"My my, that was quite the feat." Leen sauntered over to me, admiring the wreckage as she strolled. She was right. I wondered how I had even had any trouble against the Manta Phrase. This almost felt too easy.

Leen picked up two pieces of the dead Spider Phrase and lightly tapped them against each other. After that, she firmly smacked the two fragments into each other. They shattered like glass.

What's happening?

"It seems that a Phrase's body is about as brittle as glass. What a shame... I thought we'd be able to construct fine weaponry from it."

Hmph... She had a point. If we had a weapon that could rival the firmness of a Phrase's body, then even Elze or Yae would be able to go toe-to-toe with one. Well, it seemed that any and all toughness drained from a Phrase upon death. I wonder if we can harvest it for window panes or something...

"Hey Leen, what makes these guys so tough in the first place...? Could it be they're using fortification magic or something?"

"...Oh, that could be it! Magical defense by using magic as a defense?! If we operate under the assumption that the Phrase have special attributes that let them take in magic and apply them for personal benefit, then..." Leen picked up another two fragments in her hands. This time, she closed her eyes to channel some magic into the pieces, then struck them firmly against each other. A noise echoed out, but the pieces remained intact.

"Amazing, it's as I thought… The Phrase's body itself is almost like a spellstone. But what differentiates it from a spellstone is that the Phrase is much more adept at taking in magical power. They're almost one hundred percent efficient at absorbing magic, even! I had no idea of the potential involved here…"

"I don't fully understand. Lay it out for me a bit." Leen was blabbering about something I didn't fully get, but what else was new?

"To put it simply, if you pour magic into this material, then it will harden to a level that corresponds with the magic absorbed. It regenerates itself because it stores any excess magical power to use as reserve energy. The shell can constantly replenish until the mana inside it is drained entirely."

I have no idea how to process that… Is she saying I could create some kind of ultra-tough constantly-regenerating armor out of this? Wait, if I forge a weapon out of this thing, then it'd be indestructible so long as my mana reserves don't go empty, right? It'll probably grow heavier the more magic I pour into it, but I have **[Enchant]** *and* **[Gravity]**, *so that means nothing to me! Man, I just hit the goddamn jackpot!*

"Target Lock. Spider Phrase debris, including the tiny fragments. Invoke **[Storage]**."

"Understood. Targets acquired. Invoking **[Storage]**." The magic circle spread across the ground in a wide area, covering all places where the Spider Phrase's shell had fallen. All together, the fragments sank into nothingness like one would sink into water. With that, all the goods were recovered.

If I had only known how valuable this stuff was in the desert, I'd have collected the pieces of the Manta Phrase as well… Ah well, you can't win them all.

"Yee. Emoh." I turned around to find the tanned girl staring at me. I had no idea what she wanted now.

"I already told you, I don't speak your language!" As I pondered how to get her to understand me, Leen suddenly interjected.

"She's asking if you're the one who healed the injured."

"Wait, you can understand her?" I stared at Leen, amazed she could understand. *Maybe there's some kind of pattern to the language...?*

"You are aware that I'm older than my form suggests, are you not? There are even those in Mismede today that speak the mother-tongue of the Rauli Tribe."

Oh yeah... she did say the tribe requested aid from Mismede. There'd have to be some interpreters in Mismede's government for that to make sense.

Leen turned and talked to the tan girl.

"Hm, your name... er... Ontoh, Nomoho?"

"Pam." So then, the girl was named Pam.

It was kind of a pain having to listen to them without understanding them fully. Leen began freely talking to Pam about various things in the tribal tongue, but I had no idea what they were saying. It was a little concerning. Pam kept stealing glances at me during their conversation, sometimes with looks of amazement on her face. That was *even more* concerning.

"Ende didn't appear after all, eh?" I thought for sure he'd show up alongside the Phrase, but I was apparently wrong. Maybe I had misinterpreted his intentions, and he wasn't always gonna be around to stop them.

"It even caused a massive uproar and trashed the place, though…" I took another look at the area around me. There were tattered cloths, ruined buildings, and other remains of a once-peaceful village strewn about amidst uprooted trees and general carnage.

The villagers here seemed to make their homes up in the trees, building high in the branches. They moved from tree to tree using rope suspension bridges.

The woodland was dense here, almost like a rainforest, so the sunlight only shone through the canopy in areas where the Spider Phrase had gone on its rampage and knocked trees down.

"It seems that several people have passed away…" Lu looked over at a group of grieving women, looking rather grief-stricken herself. When I looked over at the weeping people clutching the pieces of their former friends and families, regret coursed through me. *If only I had been faster.*

"It's a shame that there's no magic to bring people back from the other side…" I muttered those words quietly, and Linze suddenly spoke up from nearby.

"That's not necessarily true. A spell like that does exist…"

"What?!" *Wait, there's seriously a way to bring the dead back? Wait, hold on, why am I so surprised? Didn't that happen to me?!*

"The highest tier of Light magic can resurrect the dead… But the consequences of doing so are grave."

Consequences? What, do you need to fulfill certain conditions or something? It's not like that one RPG where you have to donate to the church, is it? It's not like that money actually goes to God, anyway…

"To begin with, the body must be fresh. Meaning that one hour must not have passed since death. Secondly, the body must be intact. Nothing that could hinder a functional body can be present in the subject. Lastly, an obscene amount of magical power is needed. As well as an obscene amount of life force itself."

"Life force?"

"To be blunt, I'm referring to the very life that flows within a person. Resurrecting someone is no trivial feat. Through this method, the caster must stake part of their life on the line to perform the rite. There's a chance the caster could die."

That sounds really risky. I guess it's not a method anyone could employ unless they were absolutely ready to stake their life on the line for another person. But come to think of it, that might be the resolve needed to restore someone to life. In my case, the price I paid to return to life was to completely lose my old world. I don't really want to think about that matter right now, though... Makes me sad to dwell on it.

"That aside..." I'd noticed a while ago, but there were an awful lot of women amongst the tribe. I wondered where the men were. Had the Spider Phrase slaughtered all of them already? As I was pondering that, Leen wandered over and answered the very question I had been thinking about.

"The Rauli Tribe consists of only female members, and they are a warrior people. Males are forbidden here. The young warrior from earlier, Pam, is the granddaughter of the clan matriarch."

Wait what, are they like Amazons or something? I didn't expect to come across that trope around here...

From what Leen told me about the Rauli tribe, the girls headed out to kidnap men once they reached fertile age. They would then use the man for... rather obvious purposes.

If the child born from that union was a boy, he and his father would be removed from the village. If the child was born a female, the father would be expelled alone, and the tribe would collectively raise the girl. It was just how they dealt with children, it seemed.

Either way, the father was kicked out. But apparently over a hundred years ago, they would just kill the man after taking his seed, so maybe this was preferable...

As Leen told me the tale, I shivered a bit. The man inside of me was terrified, which was amplified by the fact that Pam was glaring at me for some reason. What was going on behind those eyes of hers...?

"What?" I eyed Pam from the side, and she suddenly bounded forward, leaping into the air straight at me!

"Wha—?!" She startled me, but ended up being way lighter than I expected, so catching her was fine. I was caught off-guard by the feeling of her soft skin, but in the next moment pain shot through my body, starting at my neck.

"OwwwaaaAAAaugh?!"

SHE BIT ME?! WHY IS SHE BITING ME?! IT HURTS! IS SHE A MONKEY OR SOMETHING? GET OFF ME! I moved my hand to try and wrench Pam's head off me, but she withdrew of her own volition right away.

I put my hand to my neck and sure enough, she had drawn blood.

What the hell was that?! Pam suddenly chuckled at me and turned on her heel before sprinting away. *No really, what the hell was that?!* All the other Rauli in the area who saw what had happened raised their voices in an uproar of laughter too.

"Touya, are you alright?" Linze came over and cured the bleeding wound on my neck. *Aah, it hurts like hell!*

"Seems she's taken a liking to you."

"Excuse me?!" Leen's offhand remark had me reeling. How in the hell could biting my neck until it was bleeding be interpreted as an affectionate gesture? Normally that kind of behavior was associated with hatred, right? Usually from a wild animal or a stray dog.

I couldn't believe that another person had just bitten me like that. I decided that the best course of action would be to retreat. The situation was too weird, and all the Rauli had started looking at me in a strange way as well... I had no idea what was up with that. I opened up a [Gate] and returned to Babylon. From there I picked up Cesca and Rosetta, and was back to Brunhild's castle in the blink of an eye.

"Aaaah, Master. Welcome baaaack!" Ripple was hanging halfway out of her picture frame in the middle of the landing. This kind of thing had pretty much become the norm for us at this point.

"Hey Ripple, thanks. Have I missed anything?"

"Uhm, you haaaave. We have a gueeeest!"

A guest? Really? Wonder who it could be...

"Huh, Tsubaki? What brings you here?"

"It has been some time indeed." The girls said they wanted to wash up, so I parted from them and headed to the audience room alone. Waiting to greet me there was Tsubaki, a kunoichi from Eashen. She knelt down upon the red carpet and looked up at me. She wore a white coat with a black scarf. It looked like she was quite worn out in general, indicating she had traveled far to get here. Her hair was as long and black as ever, no real change there.

"What are you doing so far from home? Are you running an errand or something?" Tsubaki was a ninja that served under Kousaka Masanohbu, one of the Takeda Elite Four. It'd be normal to assume she'd be out on a mission, but this was a considerable amount of distance to come from Eashen.

"No. My allegiance to the Takeda Clan has been formally broken. I may be asking too much by coming here, but I made the decision to join your duchy."

"What?" Tsubaki recounted her story to me. She said that once the new lord of Takeda took over, everything was a bit chaotic for a while. Even so, she dutifully served until one day Kousaka summoned her. He said to her, "If things continue as they are now, I have no hope for the Takeda Clan. You must leave with your compatriots and find another worthy house to serve." Tsubaki initially protested, but Kousaka actually ended up kicking her out. He was that confident about how grave the situation was.

"When was this?"

"Close to two months ago, I believe. After that, I began a personal journey." I was surprised by that. It seemed that Kousaka had some incredible foresight, to even predict this so far in advance… He must've been an incredible guy.

I mentioned to Tsubaki that Baba had been here recently and talked about his opinions on the matter, and she nodded in agreement.

"Indeed, because of the dire situation, Kousaka-sama had me removed…"

"But why me, of all people? Couldn't you have defected to Tokugawa or Oda?"

"Tokugawa and Oda are only feudal lords in the end. But you, Touya-san... Er, Touya-sama... you are an exceptional individual who may well become the next king of Belfast. I headed toward you thinking that you were incomparably superior! And now I find out you've already become a head of state! A grand duke! You're truly beyond mortal comprehension." During her voyage to Belfast she had heard stories about the founding of my duchy. And so, once she realized that I was the one in charge and that I was now living here, she chartered a boat across the Great Gau River all to get an audience with me.

"Well, a lot of stuff went on here too, but, uh... You really wanna work here? This isn't a big country like Belfast or anything. We're pretty fresh."

"Of course. If you'll accept me, Touya-sama, I would proudly serve under you." If Kousaka was fine with it, then I was fine with it too. Honestly, the recent increase of allies was making me a little happy. Kind of made me hopeful that the Takeda Elite Four would come and stay as well eventually.

"Very well, if you could please bring the remainder of my clansmen to your castle, I'd appreciate it..."

"Wait just a sec. Your clansmen?"

"Of course. It is my intention to have my entire ninja clan from Takeda's territory come here."

Is she serious?! Wait... sure, Kousaka said "leave with your compatriots," but seriously, relocating an entire clan of ninjas just like that?!

"Uh... how many people are in your clan, exactly?"

"If we include the children, then there are almost seventy."

"Gh...!" *Isn't that a bit much?! How'd you plan on moving that many people without me?! What if I was dead or missing or something?! I really didn't mean to accept more than Tsubaki... but I can hardly take it back now.*

"Uhh... well, about that... I don't have any issue with accepting your people into my country, but I can only really take you into my castle, Tsubaki."

"That would prove no issue. All proud ninja clansmen work standard jobs in the day-to-day. They have to make a living, after all."

...I guess that's fine, then? I remember reading something about ninjas from the olden days infiltrating other countries by getting standard jobs there and living out regular lives... Do they have the same kind of methods in this world?

My territory had a great body of water, as well as a large forest, so they could definitely get jobs as hunters or fishermen. Food wasn't a concern, but I'd probably need to think about setting up other amenities.

I'm gonna need mercantile contacts or something... If people are gonna be producing goods, then I'll need active traders. I should consult Zanac or Olba about it.

"It seems we've acquired many a new citizen today, sir."

"Sure seems that way, Laim..." I smiled wryly at my butler. Without further ado, I called my three knights into the throne room and told them not to be concerned about the large influx of ninjas. I decided to simply let them stay in the barracks for the time being, as I didn't have an army living there yet.

Just in case, I asked Lain to keep an eye out for people behaving suspiciously, not that I expected much in the way of trouble. I didn't know if that was a racist assumption, but I felt that those rabbit ears of hers would surely be able to sound out trouble as it happened.

"Master, you have a letter."

"Hm?" Just as Tsubaki left, Cesca came in with a small letter in hand. I had given most of my contacts a small Gate Mirror to immediately get in touch with me, so I wondered who had sent it...

I took the letter and skimmed it over. *Wow, this timing sure is convenient to the plot.*

"Who sent the letter, sir?" Laim inquired as I finished reading. I passed the letter over and told him to take a look.

"Goodness me..."

"Yup. Seems we'll be getting even more residents soon." The sender was none other than Kousaka Masanohbu himself. It had come through the Gate Mirror that I had handed to Baba recently.

It was a formal account detailing the fact that the lord of the Takeda Clan had royally messed up. He had neglected his people, failing to prevent many crimes. The people ended up making quite a ruckus, and it was a full-blown riot in some areas. Ultimately, the emperor of Eashen had to step in and formally disband the Takeda house. Its former territories were divided up between Oda and Tokugawa.

Well, that didn't take long. And he had such promise after the situation with Kansukay, too... That sucks. He had a lot riding on his shoulders and a lot to live up to, but he really should've kept his head down and tried harder. Maybe he was just acting out because of the pressure of having such a famous father. Or maybe he was just an idiot... At any rate, he's a nobody now. Apparently he had to report to the capital and face justice. He'll probably be exiled.

The most important thing here was that the Elite Four had all talked with one another and decided their services would be better held in Brunhild.

I was more than happy to have such talented people on my side. I wondered if I should consult Kousaka about the mercantile issue

I'd been wondering about earlier. I had yet to actually meet him, so I was curious about what kind of person he was.

Well then… I guess I should go meet him. With that thought, I opened up a **[Gate]** to Eashen.

"Repair the roads first. A town cannot develop without a road." Kousaka looked at the map of Brunhild, and only had that to say.

Kousaka was clearly younger than Baba, but he was still over sixty. He had a gentle face, but it was one clearly weathered by wisdom and age. He also wore his hair in a top-knot. The aura of experience and awareness emanating from him was just what I'd expect from a man who personally advised Takeda Schingen.

After I received the letter, I went straight to meet with Baba and the other Elite Four members, but they had a surprise for me.

Apparently several members of the Takeda Army who had now been displaced were willing to join my duchy. It was likely that they were troops who were extremely loyal to the Elite Four or something. There were only around fifty of them, but there was no way I could bring them in and hire them. We didn't even have any way of generating revenue yet, so paying the salary of an army was out of the question.

I briefly considered using the workshop to mass produce products for sale, but quickly decided against it. If we ended up dependent on the exports and the workshop broke down or something, we'd be done for.

"If I use Earth Magic, I can probably create a road pretty fast…"

"A functional road that leads to both Regulus and Belfast is of the highest importance. Please make one immediately. But on the other hand, Touya-sama… Er, milord. Don't involve yourself too directly in the affairs here. If you, as their lord, do too many things for the people, they may grow too dependent. It's best to only interfere directly in situations where the people cannot do it on their own."

Is that how it is…? I guess he has a point. People tend to sink into complacency pretty fast. It'd be bad for a country so young to start stagnating.

"Now, the eastern part of the nation will be set aside for agriculture. We can dig out canals to draw water from the river, then create various rice paddies. I do hope the soil there is as fertile as it is here in Eashen. With that we can begin trading with merchants and creating income for the country's administrative procedures…"

So you're saying we need to think about taxes, farmers, and sales of produce…

Honestly, I didn't think I needed to tax the people. I made more than enough money to support my growing family through adventuring alone. Still, Kousaka told me that if I didn't have taxes, the infrastructure of my government would falter. I decided that I would entrust the situation to him, but I did tell him to keep the taxes as low as possible.

"It would be good if we could export some kind of unique specialty. However, this land originally belonged to Regulus and Belfast, so it's unlikely there's anything of value around here. We may have to invest in technology to keep people drawn to us in trade."

"For the time being, I can manufacture some bicycles. It should help us earn some income to begin with, at least… Then, after a while, other countries might reverse engineer and make their own." Bikes were pretty handy and unique in this world, but they were still inferior to horse-drawn carts for carrying stuff, and regular horses still beat them in terms of speed. Still, there was an undeniable demand for bikes, so I figured they'd take off if they were mass produced. That being said, I didn't think any other nation would be able to make bikes quite as nice as mine.

"Anyway, let's try doing what we can for the time being. I'll entrust you with agricultural and business administration for the time being, Kousaka. If it doesn't work out, we can think of something else from there." After my talk with Kousaka finished, I headed over to the training ground. My three knights were being put through the wringer by Baba and Yamagata, as usual.

Since we still hadn't formally created a knight order or anything like that, I had asked the two of them to step in as instructors.

"Hey there, squirt. You done talkin' with Kousaka?"

"You're technically a vassal of mine now, Baba. Isn't it about time you stopped calling me that?"

"Don't be such a hardass. I'll call ya 'milord' and such when the situation calls for it. I got enough social decorum to know when it's needed." Baba laughed loudly and slapped me on the shoulder.

Damn it... There's just no winning with him, is there?

"Baba-dono might not change, but I'll be sure to address you right, Chief!"

"Yamagata, all ya did was stop callin' him Touya and start callin' him chief."

"Chief's good, isn't it? Sounds pretty important to me."

Well, I guess they could've used worse terms. Good grief... I'm not really good at dealing with these two, but I guess that's not so bad.

"I'm planning to go out and grab some supplies, since it's already noon. I was thinking of having Lain and the others accompany me, since it could double as a training exercise."

"A hunting trip? Sure, but do you think they're in any state?" Yamagata pointed over at the trio. They looked exhausted. Only Nikola was standing. It seemed like he was a young guy with a pretty strong will. The other two were collapsed on the ground. Nikola's fox-ears were still drooping, though.

"Come forth, Light. Breath of Vigor: [Refresh]." After the incantation, a soft light fell upon the three. Within a few moments, they hopped up, ran around a bit, did a few jumps, and swung their weapons with renewed energy.

"I'm not tired anymore...!"

"Was this your magic, milord?"

"G-Gah... I'm not worthy! I'm not worthy, milord!" It was my fatigue restoration spell, **[Refresh]**. It didn't cure injuries or heal illnesses, but it got rid of physical fatigue and restored stamina. If used, it restored people to peak efficiency, as if they'd had a good rest. It didn't change the fact that these guys had definitely overdone it today, though. I didn't want to have to use the spell too often.

"Man, our chief's really a crazy guy..." Yamagata called me crazy, but I think it was a compliment.

"Now then, let's get lunch. What do you guys feel like hunting? We could go for fowl, boars, crab..."

Everyone suddenly yelled out crab in booming voices, so it was unanimous right away. That was easier than I had expected. Bloody Crab was on the menu that night. One was about the size of a truck, so I figured that hunting two was fine if I wanted to feed everyone.

"Oh, let's be careful when we hunt the Bloody Crab, alright? It's regarded as a Red Rank monster on the guild system."

"What?!" The three of them seemed shocked, but that wasn't too surprising. Red rank was the best most could hope to reach, so it was only natural for them to be shocked.

"But don't worry too much. The two old timers here will be helping you hunt it, so you'll be just fine."

"We're what?!" I smiled inwardly. *You two didn't think you'd be getting out of this, did you?*

Once the hunt was over, I lamented over how easy it was. I defeated one of them solo using [**Gravity**]. It took me about one minute.

I left the second to the other five guys, just sitting back and watching, but I couldn't just watch for too long, so I ended up supporting them with basic magic blasts and restoration spells.

They fought with all their might for a solid thirty minutes, and the Bloody Crab finally fell. It was pretty hard for them. I should've considered the fact that none of them knew magic. That carapace on the crab was pretty damn tough, after all. I should've gone for a monster that was more suited to their attack style.

"G-Good work…"

"Ch-Chief… you're incredible… Goodness me… You're actually a monster…" Yamagata looked toward me, his tired eyes flickering with… what looked like fear. *Don't be so rude!*

The two ex-members of the Takeda Clan were still standing, but their breathing was ragged. Lain and the others, on the other hand, were almost completely worn out.

Just like before, I cast [**Refresh**] to bring them back from the brink of exhaustion.

The two old men were definitely the real deal, taking out a Red Rank monster was no small feat. The three warriors with them were also considerably tough, having held out so long.

I put both of the crab corpses in [**Storage**], then took us right back to the castle. From there, I went to the barracks and took the crabs out.

That reminds me... do we have enough condiments and seasoning? If I remembered right, we had a limited amount of miso, salt, soy, and other such things, so we'd be fine for the time being. Still, I made a mental note to hurry up with the mercantile access route.

I left the job of harvesting the crabs to the old folks and the other guys. Then, I headed off to build a highway that would stretch across to Belfast and Regulus.

Due to my territory originally being fraught with danger, the current road stretched around in a massive detour. It was down to me to build a new highway that passed through Brunhild.

It'd make the journey between Belfast and Regulus a much safer and shorter one. I decided to leave the original highway where it was, so people still had the option of bypassing my country if they felt like it.

"Maybe I should set up a checkpoint on the border or something. It'd be a whole heap of trouble if some bad guys tried coming through..." I decided to connect the checkpoint to the existing road as well. That meant I'd have to modify the existing road between Belfast and Regulus, just a little bit, but it'd be fine since I had permission to build a road from both countries anyway.

I used [Gate] to appear on Regulus' side of the territory.

"Wonder if I can connect this side to Belfast in one go... It'd be better if I could make a single one-shot straight road instead of a twisty, winding mess..." I used Earth magic to flatten the ground and smooth it out from Regulus to Belfast. Honestly, it was already enough for it to pass as a road, but I decided that it would be a bit lazy to leave it at that, so I paved it with smooth stone so carriages could come across it with ease. That would also help it stay intact during rainstorms.

After that, I built two basic checkpoints at the Regulus border and the Belfast border. I'd have to come back later and make proper ones. I then applied the finishing touches, including signposts. The signs read "Duchy of Brunhild, this way!" I figured that was enough.

Even with that set up, there wasn't exactly much that would make travelers want to head toward Brunhild. The castle could be seen from the road, but it wasn't really enough to make the average wanderer say "Hey, I should go check that out!"

Still, it wasn't like my castle was a tourist attraction or a revenue generator anyway, so I decided to put Tsubaki's ninja clan to work. I liked the idea of them manning something like a rest area, with food and drink. That way it could become a hub of gossip and information in the middle of two major kingdoms. Ideal for ninjas to work at if you asked me.

That reminded me, I needed to make a road connected to my castle, too. I went and made a stone road that stopped at my castle gates. It was a simple repeat of the previous process, just on a much smaller scale.

As I reached the castle, a pleasant smell wafted through the air. *Smells like crab stew... Man, I'm hungry.*

It was decided that our new recruits would be taught how to make bicycles in the afternoon.

I wasn't going to be the teacher, though. That task fell to Rosetta. Mostly because she knew the details way better than me. It was better to leave it to her, after all. She began teaching everyone how to make them from scratch, without magic. That girl was definitely the terminal gynoid of the workshop for a reason. If she were an engineer in my world, she'd truly be of the highest tier.

I entrusted Rosetta with the manufacturing process, and then decided to teach people how to ride some. After all, if nobody could ride them, then nobody would buy them!

As I was teaching the ninja adults, their children mistook my bikes for toys, which wasn't too unreasonable, so I ended up making a bunch of kid-sized bikes for them after they hounded me.

The grown-ups and children alike mastered the art of bike-riding in mere minutes. Their balancing skills were on point… The ninjas of Takeda were a terrifying force indeed.

"Hoh, it's really starting to take shape, huh?"

"I know, right?" As I admired the shops lining the highway, old man Naito nodded in appreciation.

Naito Masatoyoh, once one of the elite of Takeda, was in charge of everything in this area. Nothing about his appearance really stood out. He just looked like a regular old worn-out businessman.

Currently, there was nothing but a cafe, a bicycle shop, a weapon shop, an armor shop, and a general store, but it definitely had the look of a shopping district.

Further away from the highway, some houses were being built for the citizens. Actually, I had assumed the shops and houses would be built in an Eashen style, but that wasn't the case. They were all brick buildings just like in Belfast or other western countries.

"If we emphasized our foreign culture, it'd make people feel a little cautious," old man Naito said.

Travelers would drop in to visit every now and then, so the place was off to a pretty good start. The weapon shop stocked some rare and unusual swords for the area, as well as some shurikens. The cafe menu included some Eashen cuisine, as well as roll cakes, ice cream, pudding, and french fries.

Some rich customers would even buy bicycles on a whim, so business must've been booming. If business kept up at this rate, the place would be a huge success. That said, there weren't that many citizens living here, so the place probably could've managed even without business being too prosperous. As I considered the place's future, a former Takeda soldier rode up to us on a bicycle.

"My lord, a merchant claiming to be your acquaintance has arrived at the checkpoint."

"A merchant? What was their name?"

"He identified himself as Zanac the clothing merchant."

Zanac, huh? He must've come a long way to get here from Reflet.

"Okay. Let's go." I opened up a **[Gate]** and passed through to the checkpoint on the Belfast side along with the soldier.

There, I saw a horse-drawn wagon loaded with unfamiliar clothing, and Zanac, who was clad in that very same style.

"Yo, long time no see. Whoops, I guess that's no way to talk to a grand duke, is it?"

"It's fine. Welcome to the Duchy of Brunhild." He was the first person to show me kindness in this world. The fact that I became a duke didn't change that. I shook Zanac's hand before speaking up.

"So, what brings you to this country? Business with the empire?"

"That too, but my primary goal is to establish trade with this country. I would like to set up a branch store here. 'Fashion King Zanac: Brunhild,' seems fitting." Ah. That made sense. That'd be a pretty big investment, though. We weren't even sure people would come, so his idea seemed odd.

"The way I see it… this is your country. If you built it, they will come. Meaning there's no disadvantage for me if I secure an ideal location while the iron's hot." So that was his rationale. I had my doubts that a clothing store would do well at our current stage, but it would've been a problem not to have one. After all, clothes would get dirty and torn quickly and easily in the construction and agriculture rush, so honestly, it was a huge help to have a clothing store.

We returned through the [Gate] to the center of town and I introduced old man Naito to Zanac. The two of them worked out the land lot, the construction costs, the laborers and artisans, and other various business-related matters. I wasn't an expert in those topics, so I let them handle it amongst themselves.

Anyway... a branch store. Zanac was a real go-getter. He managed to expand all the way from Reflet. Though he did have some of my help.

Speaking of Reflet, I wondered how Dolan and Micah were doing. *Hold the phone. It took me a while to realize it, but this country doesn't have an inn yet, huh? Honestly, I only really thought of this place as a passing point, but travelers and merchants will need a place to stay, right? Hmm... an inn sounds like a good idea. I'd prefer an inn that incorporates a restaurant and an information exchange area, too. Guess I'll need professional help, after all.* I decided that I might as well ask.

"So, I was thinking of requesting a Silver Moon branch be built in my country."

"...Another request out of nowhere, eh." Dolan crossed his arms and sighed. That made sense. I also realized it was a sudden request.

"We'll handle the inn's construction. I want you guys to be in charge of its management. By that, I guess I mean I want to hire you as a manager."

"So that's what you mean by a branch...?" Dolan tilted his head. *Well, let's not get too bogged down by the details.*

"So, you saying you want Micah to come to that little branch then, huh?"

"Why not? I wanna go! It sounds fun!" Dolan covered up Micah's mouth with an arm to the side as I sat across the table from them in the Silver Moon's restaurant. It looked like Micah was ready to hop on board.

"Hmm... But it'll be tough here without Micah, you know?"

"Oh, is that so? You can just ask Tania for help, can't you? You have plenty of spare hands as it is already."

"H-Hey, you know how that woman is...!" Dolan suddenly burst into a panic. Tania certainly was something. She was that widow who lived on the north side of town. She'd greeted me several times. But... was she really that close to Dolan? I had no idea.

"Wouldn't it actually be better if I'm out of the way? Actually, can you even really refuse when the leader of an entire country asks you directly for help?"

"Gh...! Fine, I get it! Go already! Just don't come crying back to me!" Micah pumped her fist upon getting Dolan's reluctant consent.

I wanted to furnish the inn with a bathhouse, but there was a slight problem there... Getting the hot spring water from Belfast. It would've been improper to just take something from another country.

Brunhild had a waterway, so I just needed to find a way to heat the water from there. It wouldn't have the same effect as a hot spring, but it should have been sufficient for a bathhouse. I could blend in some [Refresh] and [Recovery] into the water, after all.

For the time being, I took Micah back with me to where old man Naito was in Brunhild.

"Oh, if it isn't Micah. Are you setting up a Silver Moon here, too?" Old man Naito had been talking to Zanac, but looked over this way with a smile.

"I decided to create a state-run inn, so I brought over a manager."

"Oh, I'm a little envious. If you would like to have employee uniforms made, then kindly keep my store in mind."

"You're a good businessman." Micah smiled as if she had thought Zanac was joking. I didn't think it was a joke, though… Those were the eyes of a predator on the hunt.

I had old man Naito and Micah plan out the inn's location. Since it was going to be state-run and all, I decided it'd be better to make it on the large side. We'd need enough space for a bathhouse too, anyway. I told Micah that I was going to prepare a room for her, so she should come to the castle later. Then, I left. As I strolled through the street on the way to the castle, children on tiny bicycles headed my way.

"Ah, milord! Hello!"

"Hello! Milord!"

"Yes, hello." The kids greeted me as they zoomed past. They sure seemed energetic. It was a good thing they liked those bicycles. It was hard to believe that those innocent little kids came from a shinobi lineage.

I saw the kids off, and soon enough, I found a familiar girl running my way with something in hand.

"Touya!"

"Oh, Lu. What's wrong?" Lu gasped for air as she handed me what she was holding. *A two-tiered lunchbox and a thermos?*

"Here's your lunch. Since you weren't back by lunchtime and all…"

"Ahh… I haven't eaten yet, now that you mention it." I took the lunchbox and headed to the shadow of a tree beside the road before pulling out a table and chairs out of [**Storage**].

I opened up the lunchbox to find rice and a variety of side dishes like a meat and vegetable stir-fry, sauteed burdock root, beef and potatoes, some layered omelets, and boiled fish in soy sauce. The food was a little misshapen, though.

"Huh? Did Crea not make this?"

"Ah, actually… Well… I made it. Crea said you liked Eashen cuisine, so I had Tsubaki teach me some of it… It's my first attempt, so it might be somewhat awkwardly done, though…"

"Hoh." It was pretty well done considering it was her first time. I used my chopsticks to try some of the beef and potatoes. Yup, it tasted just about right.

"It's good. I can't believe it's your first attempt."

"Really?! That's great!" Lu was bursting with joy. She was kind of overdoing it, honestly. She had a pretty wide range of expressions, come to think of it. But that part of her was cute. Yumina and Lu were usually quite elegant and dignified, so it was charming to see them act like girls their age from time to time.

"…Is something wrong?"

"Hmm? Nah. Just thinking about how cute you are."

"Hweh?!" Crap. I'd said it out loud. I kept eating, trying my best not to look at Lu's blushing face. I was just kind of embarrassed, but the food was good. The fish and other dishes had quite a pleasant taste.

"U-Uhm, Touya, is there any food that you hate?"

"Hmm? Not particularly. Oh, but I'm not really good with really spicy things, I guess." Elze's super spicy chicken was hell to eat… I didn't think anyone but Elze could stomach it.

"What about foods you like?"

"Hmm… It's gotta be Japane… I mean, Eashen food, I guess. Anything that goes with rice, really… Ah, I really like the taste of this beef. It's the best."

"Th-Thanks…" Her face turned red again after I praised her cooking. Must be tough.

"I've had an interest in cooking ever since I was little, but the castle workers never let me try… Every day has been just so much fun ever since I met you, Touya." Well yeah, I mean, she was a princess. There was no way they'd let her cook. That said, it was a shame to let such talent go to waste.

After I finished eating, I put the table and chairs back in [Storage] before we headed out back to the castle.

Lu kept glancing my way as she walked beside me. She'd reach her hand out and pull it back in, reach it out, and pull it back in. And so, I reached out and took her hand instead.

She twitched in surprise, but then clasped my hand back.

"Eheheh." Lu smiled shyly as we returned to the castle, hand in hand. We probably looked just like siblings. Well, we weren't in any hurry. I was sure that one day we'd look like lovers, or even husband and wife. Because I wanted to live with her in my country, forever.

Construction began on the Brunhild branches of Zanac's clothing store and the Silver Moon inn, so the shopping district started looking more and more like a shopping district. Materials were running short, but I knew we'd find some way to cover it.

Fortunately, the dearth of citizens meant there wasn't much to worry about concerning the food supply. The forest had edible plants like berries and mountain yams to be picked, as well as wild animals like boars and rabbits. There were plenty of fish in the river, too. Just as the Belfast and Regulus royals had said, this land appeared to be rather fertile. Though I guess that was why the place had a monster problem.

Well, you could say the place was, for the most part, suitable for establishing a new nation. Tsubaki suddenly came in with some new information.

"My lord, I have received word that something resembling those transporters you mentioned was found in the Elfrau Kingdom, which spreads north of the empire to the frigid tundra of the east." That was interesting. Sounded like that information came from a merchant from Elfrau. There seemed to be a mysterious cylindrical object hidden in a cave blocked off by ice, just as it was with the desert ruins. Though, the shape was different this time.

If that doctor had only been consistent, it would've been simple to look for them using search magic. I mean, I did try using the search keyword "transporter." Since the outer appearances changed each time, these things would only ever be recognized as "ancient ruins." I was starting to think the doctor just hated me.

Well, it wasn't as if the thing in the cave was guaranteed to be one of those teleporters.

Still, it must've been tough to have noticed it. Ninjas are really great. Information gathering was probably their specialty.

"Now you can obtain another doll for your collection, Master."

"…It's depressing to think that I might get more like you." I wryly cracked back at Cesca's utterance.

I had always thought this, but I got the feeling her personality was a slice of the doctor's personality. After all, some of the ones like Rosetta seemed to have some pretty artificial attitudes. Cesca, on the other hand, liked to make dirty jokes.

For the time being, I had Tsubaki show me the object's location on the map… It was pretty far. It was almost all the way up north. It'd probably be cold up there.

"Rosetta, Cesca, go on ahead with Babylon. If it gets cold, just go inside the house on the garden, okay?"

"No need to worry. Babylon deploys a barrier that maintains a moderate temperature, so heat and cold are no concern." I thought about it, and it wasn't that hot when we were in the desert, either. Seemed Babylon had multipurpose air conditioning. That sure was convenient.

Perhaps it was a vital function for the plants in the garden, actually. I mean, there could be seeds sensitive to the heat or cold.

After I sent out Cesca and Rosetta, I passed on the news about the transporter to Leen, who jumped for joy. I didn't need to tell her about it directly, but if I didn't, it would've surely proved to be scary later on.

Everyone went back to their rooms to prepare for a trip to an extremely cold area. I was fine since I had my coat. After all, my coat was imbued with anti-cold, anti-heat, anti-blade, anti-fist, and anti-magic attributes. It wasn't really that hot in the desert either, so I figured I'd probably be fine.

We brought Kohaku with us this time, but Kokuyou and Sango requested to stay on house duty.

"We're weak to the cold. It's not that we freeze completely, but we'd rather pass."

I see. It's understandable since they're a snake and a tortoise. Poor things. Good thing humans aren't that frail.

...I was too naive. I underestimated the extreme cold. How could it even have been so cold? Had the coat's anti-cold attribute worn off?! I started shivering as soon as I set foot on the snow-covered territory of Elfrau. Just how many degrees below zero was it? Meanwhile, everyone else calmly looked around. What was the meaning of this?!

"H-How are you all okay? A-Aren't you cold?"

"I'm using warmth magic. We're all at room temperature except for you." Leen gave away the trick to her little prank. It was so unfair. Why would she single me out?

"Weren't you the one who said you were perfectly shielded from the cold?"

I know, I did! I'm sorry I overestimated myself! So put your magic on me too, please!

"Come forth, Fire! A Cozy Cloak Scatters Down: [Warming]!" Leen's magical light enveloped my body. The chill calmed down immediately.

To test the magic, I picked up some snow. It didn't feel all that cold, but it didn't rapidly melt, either. It seemed that the magic didn't simply raise body temperature, but perhaps acted more like a defensive barrier against the cold instead.

Now that I was no longer distracted by the cold, I started to look around. Hidden by the pine trees was a large icy hole in the side of a mountain. The ice-covered cave continued endlessly underground. The ancient ruins we were looking for were apparently back there.

We stepped into the cave. Despite the effects of [**Warming**], I could almost swear I felt a chill run through my spine. We illuminated the cave with [**Light Orb**] and slowly made our way deeper.

"Watch your footing…"

"Take it nice and easy…" The very moment I reminded everyone to be careful, I slipped and fell on the ice. It hurt like hell. I guess it could be considered divine punishment. Perhaps I had slipped my enemies one too many times.

"What are you doing, Touya?"

"Are you okay, Touya-dono?" Elze and Yae reached out their hands and helped pull me up. If only I had shoes that would never slip. If I did the reverse of slip magic, would it let me stand on ice without slipping? Despite the slippery footing, Paula hastily descended into the icy hole. She tripped and tumbled along the way, so I couldn't help but wonder what she was even trying to do.

Afterward, we paid even more careful attention to the cave. We almost slipped again and again, but eventually made it safely to the bottom without tumbling.

"…Sure is deep." Linze muttered as she looked up. Inside the icy hole was a tall and wide cave, with icy stalagmites and stalactites clinging to the floor and ceiling. The cave was so dark that we couldn't tell where anything was. Kohaku led the way, alongside the orb of light. I put the tiger up front to detect any sort of scent or sound ahead.

"My liege… Something is up ahead. I believe it is the ruins, but it looks like there'll be some trouble…"

Huh? Found them already? Kohaku was pretty useful in the dark. I was surprised that big cat had such acute senses… But what sort of trouble did he mean? After a little cautious walking, I found out exactly what Kohaku was talking about. The black cylindrical object was covered in an enormous amount of ice. It seemed to be a wall of permafrost. A wall of ice inside a cave, and inside the ice was a black cylindrical artifact.

"It's frozen solid... Can we even put a dent in this...?" I tried shooting one of Brunhild's bullets into the ice, but it simply bounced right off. Typical. It figured it was going to be tough to crack this cold one open with the girls.

"Leen... Can you melt this with magic?"

"Hmm... I'll try, but..." Flame spewed out of Leen's finger like a flamethrower, but it was not enough to melt the ice. Why?

"Guess it's really not going to work. This isn't any ordinary ice. It's magice."

"Magice?"

"Ice that naturally accumulates magic. It can't be broken without immense force, and not even magic can melt it easily." Well, that was a pain. I was thinking of using [Gravity] to smash it, but it could've broken the artifact inside, too. Couldn't use [Gate] to move just the ice, either, since it was stuck to other places.

So perhaps melting it really would be the best option? No, but melting it with heat could've made the cave itself collapse. The main question among us was what to do next.

"Hmm, is there no good way?" I tried putting my hand on the ice wall. It was cold. And that was even with the mitigating effects of [Warming]. Normally, it would've probably been enough to freeze my skin off.

"Man, and it's right there, too."

"We could reach it easily if we could dig a tunnel..."

"A tunnel…? Ah!" The word Yumina muttered sparked a flash of inspiration. I focused magic power into the palm of my hand. That was always an option, after all.

"[Modeling]!" The ice warped and caved in in front of me. It spread out past my sides, forming a tunnel.

If we couldn't melt it or smash it… then all we needed to do was reshape it. After all, our goal wasn't to remove the ice. It was the same trick I used to bust the old guys out back in Eashen.

I reshaped more and more of the magice. Eventually, the cylindrical object appeared from within the ice.

"Now then, let's take this back to Babylon and figure out if it can teleport…"

"It sure is big." Lu was right. The cylindrical artifact was about six or seven meters in diameter and three meters tall. It was almost like a giant tuna can.

I tried circling the object by reshaping the ice with **[Modeling]**, but I couldn't find an entrance or anything. There was nothing that looked like a door, and unlike the desert artifact, it didn't look like there was a way to slip into it by touching it.

I wondered what it could be… Since the shape reminded me of a tuna can, I recalled how tuna cans were opened. *It's from the top, right?* I transformed the ice into the shape of stairs and carefully made my way to the top, telling everyone to wait at the bottom.

There was nothing on the top of the artifact except for a single cavity in the center that was about one meter in diameter. *Is that it?* I cautiously stretched my foot out to check, and sure enough, it slipped through. So that really was the entrance. That mysterious wall that only I, master of all six elements, could pass through.

"I found the entrance. I'm going in. Everyone stay on alert. If anything happens, contact me through Kohaku." I instructed everyone down below before cautiously leaping in through the top. I pierced through the ceiling and landed inside. There I found a dim, pale light, and a magic circle with six stone pillars. It seemed this was indeed a remnant of Babylon.

I poured magic of each of the six elements into each of the six stone pillars. After all six elements had been poured, the circle began emitting a faint light. Finally, I stepped into the center and poured out some Null magic. A dazzling light engulfed me, and I vanished in a flash.

Spread before me was the standard scene I'd grown accustomed to. A beautiful expanse of trees, a bright blue sky overhead, and luscious green grass as far as I could see, with a pure stream of water running through it. It seems that I had successfully warped to a new place.

I was hoping that it'd be either the hangar or the library. The storehouse would also be quite welcome, because I'd finally be able to punish whoever was responsible for all the trouble I'd been through so far.

I walked by the water, and eventually a building became visible through a clearing in the trees. The building was around three stories tall. It was fitted with stained glass windows, and had a regal air about it, somewhat like a church. It didn't have any religious iconography on it or anything, though.

The building looked to be built with red brick, all the way to the roof. Alongside it, an octagonal building jutted upward. It looked a bit like a pagoda.

"Pretty sure this is a piece of Babylon, but…"

"You're quite right, you see. A very warm welcome to you. Welcome to the alchemy lab." I turned toward the sudden greeting and found myself face-to-face with a golden-eyed young girl. She was fairly tall, had pale white skin, and beautiful pink hair that flowed to the side in a ponytail. She looked older than Cesca, physically at least.

She wore a dark top, with a large pink ribbon about her chest. On her lower body there were black tights, and a fairly standard white skirt. Her outfit wasn't really different from the ones worn by the other two when I'd met them. There was one thing setting her aside from the other two Gynoids, however. The size of the mounds beneath the ribbon on her outfit. She was on Cecile's level at the very least...

"I'm the Terminal Gynoid of the Alchemy Lab of Babylon, you see. My name is Bell Flora. But please, call me Flora." If her name was Bell Flora, then I thought it'd make more sense to call her Bell, but... it was her call. That reminded me, Cesca's full name was actually Francesca. Maybe in their culture it was normal to call people by the latter part of their names or something.

But still, she had said we were in the lab. That meant it wasn't any of the facilities we were looking for.

"You've arrived here, you see. That means you have the same attributes as the doctor. But only a person deemed worthy can become the administrator of the Alchemy Lab of Babylon."

"I know all this already. I've already been recognized by the Terminal Gynoids from both the garden and workshop."

"The garden and the workshop? That means you've met Cesca and Rosetta, you see? My, it's almost been five thousand years... How nostalgic." Flora smiled happily and put her hands to her chest. *Jiggle, jiggle...* They both jiggled...

My eyes darted downward, staring without my consent. In that moment, I knew what had happened. She'd used magic on me! That was it. That must've been it. She'd cast a wicked hex on me!

"For those two to have accepted you, you must have the required qualities, you see… But even so, you must pass my test!" Her test? Oh, that suddenly reminded me that Cesca and Rosetta both had tests for me as well… a thought that drove a cold sweat to my brow. But it was already too late. As I was lost in thought, my body was taken advantage of. Flora grasped me by the hand, forcing my digits and palm against her spongy orbs.

S-Soft… A soft sensation spread across my hand. The sponginess, the springiness… I couldn't stop myself. Flora's sudden action had scared me, so I instinctively flexed my fingers. I'd unintentionally groped her. It was inevitable, it was unavoidable! It wasn't my fault, but even so, the deed was done. I had given her a firm squeeze.

"A-Ahh, y-you see…?" Flora's lovely voice snapped me back to reality, so I quickly realized what was going on. She had violated me, somehow!

"Wh-Wh-What the hell?!" I was in a very compromising position, so I yelled out in a flurry, but… I had to be calm, I had to be composed.

"Ufufu… You've passed the test! If you had turned into a savage beast and bent my knees back here and now, you'd have been disqualified for sure, you see!"

Beast?! What the hell is wrong with you, lady?! You just sexually harassed me, in reverse? I guess? I don't get it, but this doesn't sit right with me! Flora suddenly began to undo her ribbon, then started unfastening the buttons on her blouse. I had no idea what I was even looking at.

"Now for level two, you see... Let's see if you can hold back much longer...!"

Her breasts heaved and shuddered as they sprang forth from her blouse. My eyes couldn't process what was in front of them. Fully nude, fully uncensored, up close and personal. My eyes instinctively darted away. Why the hell wasn't she wearing a bra?

"H-Hey! Put them back in already! I'm not gonna jump you, quit it!"

"Are you sure? You could squeeze them, rub them, tweak them all you like, you see..."

"I'm quite fine, thank you! I've had my fill!" I didn't even know what I meant by that. My mouth just moved on its own, so I was spewing confused garbage. I could almost hear the doctor laughing at my flustered panic... If I had a time machine, I was sure I'd have used it to go back and show her a thing or two...

"...Very well, would you like to shove them back into my blouse?"

"I said I'm quite fine, thanks!" I yelled at her, quite irritated. Seemed that this girl contained a twinge of the doctor's personality, as well. It really ticked me off.

"I recognize you formally as a man suitable for the job. Therefore, I, Number Twenty-One, Bell Flora, hereby relinquish myself to you. Please treat me well, Master." Flora adjusted her outfit and gave me a beaming smile.

Just as I'd expected, this girl was a whole heap of trouble. Before I could even process my thoughts, she violently grabbed me by the face and pulled my lips to hers. *No, not again!*

"Augh!" Just like with Cesca and Rosetta, she swirled her tongue around the inside of my mouth. *Mmph, hey! Get off me... I— Help!* After spending a short while violating my mouth with her tongue, Flora pulled back. Not before nibbling my lower lip, though.

"Mm, genetic registration confirmed. Your genetic information has entered my system, Master. From now on, the Alchemy Lab of Babylon is yours to command, you see." I heard Flora talk to me, but I was too zoned out and exhausted to fully take in what she was saying. *Come on, lady… If you were the guy and I was the girl, that definitely wouldn't have been considered okay, would it?!*

"This is a facility that specializes in the combination of materials through magic, you see. Though we primarily specialize in medication and food, we are able to do things with other materials, if need be." I was listening to Flora explain the functions of the Alchemy Lab of Babylon to me. Functionally, it sounded kind of similar to my enchanting spell. From what I understood, it could do something similar to what I did when I enchanted the Silver Moon's hot springs with [**Recovery**], just on a much grander scale.

"So, what kind of things can you make here?"

"We can create useful items, you see. Potions that cure you of injury, for example. But we can also imbue items with certain qualities, like making plants that bear disease-resistant fruits. Plants that would pass that quality on to whoever ate it, you see." That was definitely interesting to hear. I had a feeling something like that would come in handy in Brunhild's agricultural movements.

"We are also equipped with a state-of-the-art medical facility, you see. If you were to have an arm ripped from its socket, or a leg shredded into grisly, writhing strips of red paste, we would simply grow you a new one!" I wondered if that was something more along the lines of biotechnology or life-restoring magic. I guess it dealt with science in the same way that fermenting natto, soy sauce, miso, and yogurt did. Still, her mention of selective breeding made me think it was more related to genetic modification.

I wondered if we'd be able to use this place to clone people, or create homunculi... Given that Flora, the girl before me, was a gynoid with mostly biological parts... Well, it was entirely possible that she and the others were grown here.

I decided not to think about that too much.

"Could you crossbreed an apple with an orange to make a new fruit?"

"That is indeed possible, you see. I can create an orange with the taste of an apple, as well as the inverse! I can even create a crop that fuses the flavor of both into one fruit." That was incredible, but I had no idea how it worked. I wondered if we could cross garlic seeds with rice grains, and produce the ability to grow garlic rice... One fact was clear, this piece of Babylon had some of the most bizarre potential out of the lot. Still, it was more apt to call this a kind of magical synthesis, rather than alchemy. There was nothing scientific about it at all.

"They've been modified by magic, but they're still plants, you see. How they grow will depend on the hand of the one nurturing them. The taste will likely vary based on how well they're taken care of." Well, that made sense enough to me. We'd be introducing crops that had never before been seen in the world, though... So frankly, it was unknown whether or not they'd even turn out okay. The only way to know would be to try growing them. I made a mental note to set up an experimental farm for this very purpose.

As I listened to Flora's explanation, I finally set foot in the lab itself. On one side, there was a row of glass cases of all different shapes and sizes, all lined up in a row. On the other, there were various tool cabinets and storage units. There was something that looked like a control panel in the middle of the room, and beyond that there were a ton of cylindrical cases made out of glass. They sort of looked like cryogenic pods from old sci-fi movies. I wondered if they were capsules people would enter to be treated.

"This is a gathering of the many amazing chemicals and potions the professor synthesized, you see. Most of these are medicinal, in fact."

"Amazing… So she actually researched things for the betterment of humanity…"

"She certainly did, you see. Love potions, high-potency aphrodisiacs, erotic stimulants, energy tablets, libido enhancers, sensitivity agents, fertility-guaranteeing drugs… She was amazing, you see. All of these things are of the greatest potency, and with zero side effects."

"Never mind, I take it all back!" That damn old doctor was too horny for her own good. The only kind of medication she whipped up here was for a very specific subset of people!

"The effect of this one is supposed to be beyond reason, you see. I've heard it's so strong that you'll feel as though you've died and gone to heaven…! I've never tried it myself, you see, but… i-if you'd like to indulge with me, master…!"

"For the sake of the sanctity of life, I outright refuse!" Was this some kind of sick joke? I wondered if this stuff was actually safe and without side-effects, though… Things were mighty suspicious in the lab. Well, it didn't matter much. I wasn't planning on using any of it either way… At least I probably wouldn't use any of it, yet.

"Didn't the doctor create anything, like… normal?"

"Not at all." Damn, that was blunt. This facility really was useless to me, after all… It was like a complete manifestation of whimsical nonsense. I began to wonder whether or not bringing my precious brides-to-be near this place would be a good idea…

I left the lab and bared myself to the wind, deep in thought. Well, I have no choice but to bring the others…

"The Alchemy Lab of Babylon…? Is that even going to be of any use to us?" Leen let out a frustrated mutter. Seems she was disappointed it wasn't the facility she was after.

I'd called everyone over to the new facility, then set a course for Brunhild. I was planning on linking up the new piece to our Babylon puzzle.

"Uhm… did I do something wrong, you see?"

"No, don't mind it." Flora looked over with a troubled expression. It wasn't a problem that Leen was irritated, but if she was going to get like this every time until we found the library, I decided I'd stop bringing her along. That aside, everyone except Leen was staring over at Flora.

"Ah, are you the one in charge of the lab…?"

"Ah, I'm Flora, you see."

"Th-They're big…" Both Yumina and Lu had their eyes transfixed on Flora's hefty melons.

"Wh-What's with those things?"

"I-I can't possibly win… Not against those… Th-They knock me out of the park…" The twins shuddered in misery for some reason… Yae and Leen, on the other hand, didn't seem especially troubled. Yae's bust was about the same size as Flora's anyway, while Leen seemed to be deep in thought.

I wondered why they cared so much… Well, it wasn't too hard to figure out. After all, a man tends to glance at larger things more often. In the end, I didn't care. Big or small, the chest still held the heart. Big ones were eye-catching, but it didn't matter much to me in the end.

"D-Do you prefer them big, Touya?!" Lu looked at me with wide eyes, seeming about ready to cry. That wasn't the case at all! Flora's big knockers had nothing to do with my tastes. Sure, my eyes might have occasionally darted down there, but my heart wasn't dominated by her chest.

"You should not fret, you should not. Lu-dono and Yumina-dono will surely blossom at a later date, they will. When I was your age, my bust was around the same size, it was." Yae's words brought hope to the saddened eyes of Yumina and Lu, but Elze and Linze simply sank into a deeper despair.

"...Perhaps we could make them grow with a little massage?"

"What the hell?! Don't say stupid crap like that!" I ended up overreacting to Leen's casual comment. That irritating fairy really never knew when to shut up. Upon hearing the exchange, everyone except Flora averted their eyes and blushed beet red. Flora herself only smiled widely, then opened her mouth. *What are you doing?*

"Ehehe, my dear master already massaged mine a short time ago, you see..." *Why in the world did you think that was a good thing to say right now?!* Everyone, other than Leen, turned their gazes upon me in seconds flat. Flora opened her mouth with an innocent little smile, then... dealt the final blow to her enemies with her words.

"He planted a wonderful kiss upon my lips as well, you see."

What?! You damned fiend, what the hell are you saying?! Are you taking a sick pleasure in all of this?! You're the one who kissed me! I thought I could see Doctor Babylon's wicked grin hiding behind Flora's innocent beaming for a moment there.

"Touya, I believe we need to have a small chat..." Yumina turned to me, smiling, but there was no kindness in her eyes. All of the other girls wore the same terrifying expression.

Wait, no! This is a misunderstanding! I'm innocent here! I was made to bow down and listen to all of them yell at and lecture me for some time after that. It wasn't fair... Once again, I was reminded of why hunting for the pieces of Babylon was a terrible idea.

Paula patted me gently on the shoulder, reassuring my dejected self. Only she was there to comfort my wounded heart.

The alchemy lab docked with the workshop and the garden, way up in the skies of Brunhild. At this point, the structure was around the size of a castle. It didn't really have that many buildings, though.

Cesca wore a maid uniform, Rosetta a workman's overalls. Flora, on the other hand, changed into a nurse outfit. I guess they all had their preferences for casual attire. I wasn't really sure why she made that choice of all things. But I did consider the fact that the alchemy lab doubled as a medical facility, so it wasn't too far-fetched to call it a reasonable choice of clothing.

That being said, I thought her choice of a pink nurse outfit complete with matching white stockings-and-garter belt combo was pushing it a little far. It felt more like a sexy nurse outfit than an actual uniform. Not to mention the fact that the outfit really seemed to emphasize the bust. I had no idea where to look.

Flora's medical knowledge was fairly extensive, so I decided to put a doctor's office inside the castle for her to work out of. I could pretty much heal whatever with my magic, but having an actual medical facility in-house would be a very useful emergency backup.

In the meantime, I planned to have the alchemy lab produce rice hybrids. I had acquired many rice seeds from Eashen, and the plan was to imbue them with resistance to disease and general plant-destroying trouble. I had set aside a plot of land in the eastern part of my nation, it was my experimental agricultural zone. I hoped it would work out.

The street along the highway to Brunhild was also being well developed. Old man Naito was really giving it his best, so I was quite happy about that.

The Brunhild Branch of the Silver Moon had been opened successfully too, it would prove a good place for weary travelers to rest their heads. I had set up a bath house there, too. It was proving pretty popular, on account of its fatigue-restoring properties. Micah ended up hiring a whole fleet of employees, most of which were ex-Takeda ninjas. It felt like she was really stepping into the shoes of a managerial position.

"Seems Brunhild is coming along quite nicely… quite nicely indeed…"

Clink.

"Well, it's Touya's nation, after all. I wasn't too concerned."

Clink.

"Ah, sorry, Beastking. That's Pon. Hoho…"

Clink.

"Heheheh. This is what you get for calling off me. Ron, Emperor. Tanyao, pinfu, and iipeikou. That's 3900 points." Ah, Refreese's emperor just played into the emperor of Regulus's hand. Wait, what were these guys doing here? This was Brunhild castle's gaming center. And the rulers of the western nations were all gathered around its mahjong table. But not me. I wasn't here to play mahjong.

"So, what exactly did you call us all here for?"

"Hm? No real reason. I simply wished to play mahjong with you all."

The king of Belfast responded casually. That's why they were here? I even went out of my way to use the Gate to check up on them. These guys really need to take their safety more seriously.

They pushed all their tiles into the depression in the center, and the automatic table provided them with a new fully shuffled set. They distributed the tiles with practiced movements and began their next game. They've really taken a liking to this game…

"Well, I also thought this would make for a good opportunity to exchange information." The emperor smiled as he discarded a tile. I was glad they're all getting along, but this was a little worrying. It would be a pretty big problem if all the heads of state neglected running their countries and spent all day playing mahjong instead.

"So you said you were swapping international gossip?"

"Indeed. Lately there's been a bit of a stir within the Ramissh Theocracy." The King of Belfast spoke up whilst sorting through his tiles. I had vaguely heard about the Ramissh Theocracy, it was a sovereign nation located to the southeast of Regulus. If I remembered right, it was close to Mismede, accessible by crossing the Great Gau River. You could also reach Belfast by going downstream further from there.

"What's happening over there?"

"Well they say that there's been a vampire running about Isla, their holy city."

"A vampire?" That certainly sounded strange. But, on the other hand… I might've just been out of the loop. Vampires could just be another common species in this world. I tentatively looked over to the beastking. He was a demi-human, after all.

"According to what I've heard, there's new victims every night. Each of the corpses found is a dry husk, drained of all its blood." How terrifying. This murderer certainly had questionable hobbies.

"That's why people think it's the work of a vampire... a member of the Vampiric Clan." The emperor explained to me as he dropped a tile. The Vampire Clan, huh? So there was an actual race of people known as vampires, then. Well, seeing as there was an Aquatic Clan in Mismede, it stood to reason that there would be a lot of different races in this world.

"The truly troublesome thing about this incident is that it had to be in Ramissh. Its citizens are all devout followers of Lars, the god of light. They despise denizens of the dark, no matter who they are. Anyone who so much as has an affinity with Dark magic is shunned." The beastking grimaced as he discarded his tile. Seriously? That sounded more like a cult than a religion.

"Who's this Lars guy?"

"Hm? Oh, you haven't heard of him Touya? It's an old legend about the founding of Ramissh. A thousand years ago, the land was overrun by demons and spirits. But then Lars descended from the heavens and cleansed the land of all that was evil. The people that lived there came to worship this god of light, and spread his gospel wherever they could. That was how the Theocracy of Ramissh came to be...or so the tale goes." I tilted my head in confusion at the king of Belfast's explanation. God of light, huh? I already knew two gods, so perhaps it wasn't so farfetched a story after all. I doubt the god of love had anything to do with it, but there was always the other one. Though I couldn't imagine it, really.

Besides, it seemed like he liked to avoid getting involved in worldly affairs. He had a bunch of other worlds to manage as well too, so he was probably too busy to deal with every little problem that popped up.

I could always call him up and ask, but it didn't really seem important enough to warrant it. He'd probably get annoyed if I called him up for every little thing. He was God, after all.

"Dealing with Ramissh is always so irksome. They insist on making every decision based on their holy doctrine. Everything is done 'in the name of justice and light.' They're all so stiff and uptight. Their pope especially."

"Oh yes, I cannot deal with that pope either. Any time we meet I always get a lecture. All that old crone ever does is nag. Well, I suppose she does mean well."

The emperor and the beastking exchanged wry smiles. Pope?

"Excuse me, but when you say pope, what do you mean?"

"Ramissh is a theocracy, not a monarchy. The ruler is elected from among the highest ranking bishops at the time, they don't inherit their position. Once elected, the pope rules until they die, or chooses to retire. The current pope is Elias Altra. Or rather popess. This is the twentieth year of her reign so she must be past sixty by now... Ah ha." The Refreese emperor dropped his tile onto the table.

"That's a ron, Emperor. Pinfu with two dora. 3900 points."

"Again?!" Once more, the Refreese emperor had played into the emperor of Regulus' hand. The beastking looked up at the sky in defeat.

"Ahh, I almost had a chinitsu too...Why must you keep going for quick wins with cheap hands, Your Highness?"

"Strategy, my good man. Even if I never win big, as long as I'm the only one who wins, I'll come out ahead."

The king replied triumphantly. Luck was what made mahjong such a thrilling game after all. In a way, their playstyles reflected their personalities as well. You could learn a lot about someone by how they played. The Belfast king continued talking as they pushed all the tiles into the center.

"The Vampire Clan is actually one of the few clans that make up the demonkin. They're not exactly a rare species, but they definitely know what Ramissh thinks of their kind. So it's odd that one would show up there. There's something fishy about this whole situation." It did sound like suicide for a denizen of the dark to show up there. Though if the vampire hadn't been caught yet, that meant he was doing a pretty good job of hiding. Hmm, this definitely struck me as odd…

"Well, as long as it's not affecting us there's no reason to worry about it. It's not like the entire clan has started attacking people or anything. Though if Ramissh starts going after the whole clan because of this, I'd take the vampires' side." The beastking harrumphed loudly and crossed his arms over his chest. Beastmen were still discriminated against in a lot of places. He probably hated the idea of someone being persecuted just for their race or birthplace. Though I agree it's a little fanatic to believe anyone that belongs to the dark is automatically evil.

The Ramissh Theocracy…

It didn't sound like a place I'd want to go to. I did believe in Gods, and I probably had more reason to be grateful to them than most, but I couldn't say I cared for religion.

In the end, the Refreese emperor kept losing to the emperor of Regulus, and the round ended with him in the lead. The four rulers agreed to meet again the next month and went home.

Seems they'd decided to make it a regular thing.

"Ah! I lost again!"

"Me next, milord! It's my turn!" The sounds of children playing filled the street.

I picked up the small iron top the kid had sent flying. I'd thought to make some toys for the kids.

I'd been teaching them how to spin it properly. They'd picked up on it pretty fast. There was a makeshift arena made out of a bucket with a cloth to protect the sides where the kids were having heated top battles.

Needless to say, my top was the best, and before long the kids had made it their goal to beat me. As of now, they had yet to succeed. Bwahaha, they were fools to underestimate the top spinning skills my grandfather passed down to me.

"Alright, that's all for today. Here, I'll give you all your own tops so, be good kids and go home, okay?"

"Really?!"

"Yaaay!"

"I'm gonna be your servant when I grow up, milord!"

If I could buy retainers for the price of a single top, I could probably hire an army of servants.

I watched the kids run happily home, and spotted a familiar figure standing nearby out of the corner of my eye.

A smiling old gentleman with a sturdy build and a thick white beard. There was a pair of fox ears growing out of his head, and a bushy tail sprouting from his back.

"If it isn't Olba. How long have you been standing there?"

"It has been far too long, master Touya. Or should I now address you as His Highness, the Grand Duke of Brunhild?" It was the Mismede merchant, Olba. The father of Olga and Arma, and uncle to Nikola, one of my own knights.

"I did not expect to find someone of your stature here, playing with children in the street. It was so unusual that I couldn't help but stop to watch. However..." Grinning, Olba plucked one of the tops left behind in the makeshift arena.

"This is a truly unusual toy. I have not seen its like before. And its structure is so simple. Would you be willing to let my company sell this creation of yours?"

"Yeah, that's fine. It isn't exactly something I came up with anyway, and it's not like the manufacturing methods are a secret. Though, if you could, I'd like you price it low enough that children can afford it."

"Hmm. If I kept the price that low, there would be no reason for people to buy more than one. In which case..." He really was a merchant to the core. Already, he was calculating how to maximize earnings. If he kept the price low, he'd have to sell large quantities to make a profit. So unless he had an incentive to produce in bulk, there was no point in selling it.

For other toys, you could expect people to come back for more after they broke their first one. However, tops didn't really break easily. He did have a point. In that case...

"What if I made different varieties... Wouldn't that solve our problem, making them fun to collect? For example, I could make them in different colors, put the various family crests on some, maybe images of Dragons and knights on others. Wouldn't that make kids want to gather all the different kinds?"

"That's perfect! Even if they don't break, kids will want to buy a bunch that way. If we take advantage of that... brilliant!" Maybe I shouldn't have said take advantage of. That made it sound sinister. But it was true that making them a collector's item he could produce as many as he wanted. Well kids would probably be happy with just one, and the adults that had an interest in collecting would have the money for more.

"This country truly is a wonderful place. There are so many opportunities for a merchant here. Better yet, it seems most merchants haven't discovered that fact yet!" His eyes were glimmering at all the possibilities for profit. It seemed that he wanted to open a Strand Company branch store here. And in fact, the initial purpose of his visit had been to obtain approval for that.

As they operated internationally, allowing them to establish an office here would certainly make it easier to import and export goods. There was no reason not to give him permission.

I decided to call over old man Naito and Nikola, to have them help figure out a suitable location for their store. Nikola was more of a bodyguard than a merchant, but I was sure he'd enjoy the opportunity to talk to his uncle so I decided to bring him as well.

I let Olba decide how he was going to sell the tops. For formality's sake, the country was entitled to ten percent of his profits on it.

I never expected that years down the line my top would be a highly coveted item that nobles from all over were willing to pay ludicrous sums to obtain.

"All right, I can use magic to preserve its hardness. Then, just in case it breaks, let's give it a restoration function. Now, if I [**Program**] it to absorb the surrounding magic…" Recently, I've been busy creating weaponry using the Phrase crystals we'd gathered.

After all, it was an item that changed magic into hardness. The greater the amount of magic it received, the tougher it became. It also increased its cutting ability, as well. That was the secret behind the sharpness of the Phrase's attacks.

I filled the crystal with a significant amount of magic. That allowed me to replicate the Phrase's hardness, sharpness and even its regenerative abilities.

"And that's how I made this sword. The first one of its kind. I call it 'Touka.'"

"Touka…" Yae took the colorless, translucent sword from its sheath. The crystalline blade was reminiscent of ice. The light coming from outside the workshop gave it a brilliant shine.

"Just so you know, I made it automatically absorb magic from the surroundings — primarily the air itself — so I don't think it will ever run out of that. If that ever happens, though, you should know it by how well it cuts. Just fill it up with magic and it should be back to normal." She tested its sharpness on a piece of iron I'd prepared, and the blade cut through it like paper even though she just lightly touched it. *This sharpness is borderline scary.*

"This should be able to cut through the Phrase. You have my thanks, Touya-dono." After putting Touka into its sheath — which was made of a Phrase crystal, too, but painted to not be translucent — Yae looked at me and gave me a blissful smile. That made the creation more than worth it.

However, behind her, I saw four highly familiar faces — all pouting at me.

"...I've made things for you too, so stop looking at me like that." First, with Lu being a dual-wielder, I gave her two short swords. They were pretty much just like Touka.

I didn't have any weaponry for Yumina and Linze, but I gave them both a set of Phrase crystal bullets. I set them to, upon landing, create an [Explosion] behind them, causing them to get wedged into the target.

Though the [Explosion] itself wouldn't have much effect, it worked pretty well as a propellant. I also made the bullets sharp and used magic to increase that sharpness even further. The idea behind it was based on a fictional weapon that used explosives to launch a high-speed metal stake — the pile bunker.

Then there were Elze's gauntlets, which made good use of the crystals' toughness.

I'd spent some time thinking on how I could make their power more focused, and I'd ended up adding some brutal-looking, cone-shaped attachments on the fists. Two sharp horns — left and right — focused on a single point. It was easy to imagine just how destructive a hit from those would be...

Normally, they would be hidden inside the back of the gauntlets, and I made it pop out when she made her fists face forward — a sort of "pulverize mode," so to speak.

"Just so you know, it's dangerous to use it outside of battles, so don't keep it in that state when—" Suddenly, a crash. Right as I was saying that, the stone spread out on the workshop grounds was pulverized. *Damn it! I know you want to try them out, but that's gonna make Rosetta cry!*

"Not bad. Breaking things is much easier than normal."

"That's because I've made it that way... Ahh man..." As I was thinking of what excuse I'd make when Rosetta saw what happened here, I heard the sound of trees falling down.

"Impressive sharpness."

"Amazing! The trees are so large, yet they get cut like radishes!" As Yae and Lu turned gleeful due to the effectiveness of their blades, I looked at the fallen trees and concluded that no excuse would work now.

Guess I'll bite the bullet and get scolded... I'm sorry, Rosetta. It's odd, though. How did it come to this? Yumina and Linze, too, were putting the bullets into their gun chambers, so I somehow got them to stop. I couldn't allow the casualties to increase. *Why are my wives so keen on fighting? Good grief.*

After testing the weaponry, we made our way back to the castle, where we were met with a panicked Lapis. *Did something happen?*

"Sir... No... Your Highness. You have messengers from another country. Please get appropriately dressed and go to Kousaka." *Eh? Messengers? That's a first. I wonder what country they're from...* My Duchy of Brunhild was gradually becoming a proper country. Naturally, international relations were next, but I haven't made any preparations for this.

My country was surrounded by Regulus in the east and Belfast in the west. That meant that there was no chance of me getting invaded as long as I was on good terms with these two countries.

However, that didn't mean that not getting along with other countries was a good idea. Every nation had their motives and methods, and there was always the possibility that they could do something indirectly.

Still, so far, not a single nation considered my new, small country to be worth interacting with. The countries in the western alliance knew me very well and I interacted with them often. However, I didn't know how to react if the messenger came from a country I didn't know.

"It is a pleasure to finally meet you, Your Highness, Grand Duke of Brunhild. I am Nesto Renaud, a messenger sent here on behalf of Elias Altra, Pope of the Ramissh Theocracy."

"And I am Phyllis Rugit."

"Very well." I sat on the throne in my throne room. Kousaka — the ex-Takeda Elite Four member — was standing next to me and throwing me glances.

I know, I know. I have to avoid saying much and leave most of it to you. After all, we didn't know what they wanted. Rather than saying something unnecessary, it was better to just stay silent. "Silence is golden," as they say. Also, I had little of the so-called "majesty" about me; I had to be considerate so they wouldn't underestimate me.

"We wholeheartedly welcome you. Now, might we hear what is your business here?" Kousaka spoke to the messengers. The person before me — Nesto — was a grown man with short, blond hair. He was clad in a fancy white robe with golden embroidery on it. At first glance, he looked like a priest. He appeared to be over 40 years of age. His hair seemed kinda weird, though.

The person next to him — Phyllis — was a quiet, bookish-looking girl with light purple hair in a bob cut. She looked about as old as me. Her robe was white, too. It wasn't nearly as flashy as Nesto's, though.

They looked like priests of the Ramissh Theocracy. They worshiped the god of light — 'Lars,' I believe. If they were priests there, then they had quite a lot of political power.

One of them — Nesto — spoke up.

"Our theocracy's pope — Elias Altra — wishes to befriend the Duchy of Brunhild. We also wish to propagate the Church of Lars in your lands by having you accept it as your state religion. If you are willing to do that, Ramissh Theocracy will recognize you as a sister country and always support you."

…Huh? State religion? As in, one that's protected by law?

"We invite you to undergo a baptism and begin building a church in your lands. If you follow the teachings of Lars, the god of light, your nation will surely become more prosperous than ever before." Nesto spoke those words with great zeal and enthusiasm, but I felt the exact opposite, and it only got stronger with every word spoken.

The hell's this guy saying? Why should I undergo a baptism from such a weird cult?

"The teachings of our Lord Lars destroy evil and bring forth light and justice…"

"No, thank you."

"…Huh?" My words caused him to stop his heated speech and turn stiff.

"Whatever do you mean?"

"Exactly what I said. I don't need a religion in my country." The speech dragged on for a bit, but it was basically an invitation to his faith. And honestly, I found it shady as hell. The god of light? Did he really exist?

"So you are saying that you have no need for the teachings of our Lord? Do you not believe in God?"

"I'd prefer it if you didn't say such silly things. There's not a man in this world who believes in God more than me. I thank him every day." I spoke those words as Nesto glared at me.

It's not your god, though.

Reacting to what I'd said, the Phyllis girl joined the conversation. Unlike Nesto, however, she didn't seem mad. She looked more confused than anything else.

"Then why? If you believe in God, why do you refuse to spread his word? Seems contradictory, if you ask me."

"It isn't. Also, you say that your god is the 'god of light,' Lars. Does 'light' mean that there's a god of dark? Are there any other gods?" I answered her question with another question. The one to answer was Nesto, who puffed his chest as he did so.

"God of sea, god of mountains, god of earth — certainly, there are many various gods. However, the one standing above them is the god of light, Lars — the most glorious of all. He's an absolute god of justice, and not even the god of dark can stand up to him."

"Doesn't seem like it, though."

"What?!" Nesto went past just glaring at me. His voice turned ragged as he stood up — anger palpable in his expression and demeanor.

Well, I expected as much.

"Are you saying that our Lord is powerless?!"

"You called him an 'absolute god of justice,' right? Then why are there still criminals and evil-doers?"

"Th-That's… That's what we're here for! We punish evil in His stead! It's our duty! We are His limbs and…!"

"That's just *your* power, isn't it? Nothing divine about it. Don't confuse that." Nesto's shoulders were shaking at this point. *Did I say too much? Am I wrong, though?*

"Then what has *your* God given to us?!"

"Nothing. He's pretty busy. He leaves us to take care of ourselves. Doesn't intervene unless there's something important. Also, it's not like I'm completely rejecting your teachings. If you believe in your god, it's all fine by me."

Everyone has their very own God inside their hearts. Let people believe whatever they want. It's fine like that. However, I don't like people using their Gods in international relations.

Nesto looked at me with pure hatred in his eyes.

"...It appears that you have been bewitched by a wicked God. It appears we will have to purify you."

"Ah?"

What did he just say? "Kohaku. Hold him down."

"As you command."

"Augh?!" Kohaku attacked Nesto from behind, pushed him down on the floor and kept him there with its front legs. Naturally, Kohaku was in Byakko mode.

I walked over to Nesto, crouched down and looked in his eyes — full of fear of Kohaku.

"I don't care what God you believe in. You can pray to whatever divinity you like, regardless of whether they actually exist or not. However, I won't allow you to treat my God as wicked. You don't know anything about him, so I don't want you saying stuff like that." I glared at Nesto, opened a [Gate] on the floor and teleported him... Straight to the river outside the castle.

When he disappeared, he left behind his blond hair.

I knew it was a wig.

I looked to the side and saw Phyllis, who was wordless with shock.

Oh. Crap. I overdid it.

He was a messenger from another country. I had better methods of dismissing him. Hearing him talk badly about God got to my head. *I mean, seriously, how could that nice old man be a*

99

wicked God? Still, I went too far… I turned around and saw Kousaka with his hand on his forehead, exhaling a long sigh. *Crap, I really messed up. And he told me to not talk too much, damn it.*

"Umm… Priest Nesto is…?"

"Well… I teleported him outside the castle. Don't worry, he's not hurt."

Probably wet as hell, though. Guy might even catch a cold. Not that I would care.

"My apologies. Please forgive his rudeness. Just so you are aware, this audience with Your Highness was based primarily on Nesto's own initiative, and the pope was not too enthusiastic about it." Phyllis bowed her head.

Really? "Having this country adopt the Church of Lars as its state religion would be a great achievement, after all. I believe that that was Nesto's plan."

So he just wanted to get ahead in life, huh? Pretty vulgar for a priest.

"Anyway, I don't plan on having a state religion. Tell that to your pope."

"Yes. Certainly. By the way, umm… about what you said… Have you perhaps met God in person, your Highness?"

Oh? Did I say something that gave it away? Man, how should I answer this?

"I am sorry. This must sound weird… I just… became doubtful about whether God truly exists or not…" Phyllis whispered that and brought her head down.

You sure you should be saying that? You're a priestess, aren't you?

"This question was always on my mind. People punish evil in the name of justice. While a part of me sees that as a wonderful thing, I can't help but wonder whether it's fair to mark someone as evil

100

simply because they're demonic or born from the dark. Also, can't we forgive someone who only made a single error? Such questions came one after the other and..." *I can somewhat understand her, but is it really okay for her to continue being a priestess while doubting her God so much?* Suddenly, the smartphone in my pocket began vibrating.

Eh? Now, of all times? Since there was only one person who ever called me, I knew exactly who it was.

I took it out and answered the call.

"Hello?"

"Hey, it has been a while. I take it you know who this is?"

Yeah, of course I do. Still, you should say who you are when calling. This timing, though...

"Were you watching?"

"Happened to be watching, yes. I must say, having you snap like that was quite satisfying. Thanks for getting mad for my sake."

Crap, he saw me. Damn, this is embarrassing. As I was writhing about the stuff I'd said, Phyllis fearfully called out to me.

"Umm... who are you talking to?"

"God."

"Eh?!" As Phyllis became surprised, I noticed that Kohaku — standing next to me — was in a weird state. The tiger wasn't moving a muscle.

Wait, what? Even Kousaka is completely stiff. What the hell?!

"Oh, I just stopped the time there for a bit. Things could get troublesome if anyone else saw me."

"You stopped time?! Wait, did you just say 'if anyone else saw me'?! Do you mean that...?"

"I thought that I should answer that young lady's questions. I'm coming over. She won't believe you otherwise. All right, then..."

"Hey…!"

Seriously? He actually hung up. I moved the smartphone away from my ear and looked at Phyllis.

"He's coming over…"

"'He'…? Who do you mean?"

"Well… God." As Phyllis and I were both in a state of astonishment, God descended before us, surrounded by blinding light. His divine — obviously, considering he was God — aura engulfed us. A single glance was enough to see just how celestial he was. He slowly went down and stood on the same ground we mortals walked on.

"Yoo-hoo, it is I, your man God."

"Be more serious, damn it!" *You obviously had more majestic things to say! And stop smiling like that, the situation is ridiculous enough as it is!*

Phyllis stood before the merry old man, trembling uncontrollably. After a few seconds, she seemed to lose the ability to stand. She collapsed to the ground, twitching.

"Hm? Are you quite alright, dear?"

"Uh, God…" God didn't seem to understand what was going on, so I called to him.

"There's a… force you're exuding right now, can you maybe turn it off? It's making it hard for me to even look at you, so I can't even imagine what it's doing to her."

"Oh? Ah, very well. Goodness me, I forgot I was in the mortal realm. Forgive my carelessness… Divine energy tends to leak right out of me! I didn't even notice…" Gradually, the golden shine in the room receded back into God's body. Alongside it, the horrifying feeling of submission and oppression vanished as well. That's God for ya, I guess.

"We should be quite fine now, I believe. Are you alright, dear?"

"Y-Yes…" Despite her words, Phyllis still only really seemed capable of raising her head. That was perfectly understandable, all things considered. Having been shown something like this? She'd have no choice but to admit the truth. I think her earlier question about the validity of my God had been promptly answered. God absolutely existed.

"We should change venues, I think. Is there another, more comfortable room in the area?"

"Hm? I mean, I have a meeting room…" I opened up a [Gate] and the three of us went through. Phyllis had trouble standing, so I had to lend her my arm until we reached the couch.

I went to prepare us all some tea, passing by a frozen Renne and Cecile, who were apparently laughing at something before being paused. I poured out the tea by myself into a big pot, then returned to the room with a few snacks and three teacups.

When I returned to the room, the two were much like they were when I'd left. God was swaying around a bit, looking about the room like an excited child, while Phyllis was sweating bullets and almost completely immobile. Her eyes, on the other hand, were darting all over the place.

I poured out the tea into the cups and lined the snacks up. God took the first sip, and I asked my question.

"I've got a question for you, old man."

"Mhm? What is it?" God placed his teacup down on the table with a smile, and turned to face me.

"Do you know of any god of light named Lars?"

"That… does not ring a bell. I've never heard that name, no. In fact, amongst all journeyman-level gods, and even trainee gods… there is no such being as Lars, god of light." I didn't expect him to be that confident. Phyllis looked like she had been punched in the stomach. But that was only natural, the god she had been raised to believe in had just been completely outed as fictional.

"Well, maybe he isn't called Lars. Is there a god of light?"

"No, there is no such thing as the god of light. Well, if I were forced to classify a god of light, that would probably fall under my jurisdiction. I'm the world god, after all. There's a god of wind, a god of fire, a god of dark, and so on. For the most part, deities with the 'god of' prefix are the most simple and lowest of the godly hierarchy." Hm, I wondered if that meant the god of love was a lower level God, as well. That confused me, because she seemed very friendly with my God, who I figured was pretty much at the tippy-top. I didn't really know much about the social affairs of the divine realm, nor did I care that much.

"B-But… if that's the case, then what about the legendary incident, in which High Light Priest Ramirez called down Lars, god of light?" Ramirez, the High Light Priest, was the founder of the Ramissh Theocracy. The person who supposedly purified the land by borrowing the light of God.

"Hm? You say he called upon a God? Even if humans could summon Gods, which I sincerely doubt… it would still be rather rare. Then again, there are some Gods that act upon simple whims, so I could not rule it out entirely." The irony here was palpable. This God was probably the most whimsical of the lot!

"Still, as the story goes… I do not believe it was a God. It is more likely that he summoned a spirit. To be more specific, a Light Spirit."

"That's a little ambiguous… Is it possible to peep into the past and see what happened?"

"That is not impossible, but… it would be a bit of a bother. Let me explain in terms you may understand a little better. It is quite easy to pause an episode of something if you watch it on DVD, yes? But say you recorded television for an entire year, and suddenly needed to find the advertisements of a specific late-night talk show from a year and a half ago. Your recordings are numerous, and you have not indexed them… it would be quite hard to reach that certain point, would it not?" That was a needlessly complicated explanation, but I pretty much understood.

"But then… what of our teachings? Our doctrine…?" Phyllis looked completely depressed, which was only natural given that God had just shot down her entire life. It was understandable, but even so, I didn't expect her to get that torn up over it.

"Do you people need the hand of God to hold yours? Can you not march forward for the sake of your own beliefs? Your own responsibilities? There's no harm in taking God as a piece of emotional solace, but you must not use religion as a crutch. Your parents, siblings, lovers, friends, you must trust in them, as they trust in you. To be dependent upon us is the greatest mistake you could make. The Gods will do nothing to your world. I can assure you of that. Only you are capable of saving yourselves, or destroying yourselves. You are the ones with the power change to the world, to create miracles. We above will simply watch down upon you." God was certainly being thorough, but he still interfered now and then, didn't he?

I decided to keep my mouth shut. I didn't think my commentary would have anything to add. Phyllis seemed pretty sad, anyway, so snarky commentary would just be insensitive.

"Well, even though I said that, I suppose it was not entirely the case... I typically leave you to your own devices without looking. If young Touya were not sent here, I may not have taken a look at affairs for another ten thousand years or so." Just like that, he completely ruined the beauty of his message! Even though he had made a point to say the Gods were watching, it felt more like they were neglecting! He probably had a ton of different worlds to manage anyway, so keeping an eye on every one would be a pain. "Is that truly the case?"

"Indeed. It may sound somewhat cruel, but the world is not my responsibility. No world is. The inhabitants are the ones who decide what happens to their world. The Gods will do nothing, I promise you that. Well, we would interfere if the troubles in the world were caused by us, for example the rare incident of a God turning wicked and laying waste to the world below. We would step in then." I certainly hoped nothing like that happened to us. Sounded like a bad time for everyone. The rules seemed a little flexible and contradictory there. Gods sure were whimsical.

"If I were to summarize, I'd say that I want the people of their respective worlds to deal with the problems of their respective worlds. Even if a great Demon Lord appeared and began to wage war upon the world, hoping to crush or dominate it, we Gods would do nothing if the Demon Lord were a natural resident of the world to begin with. That being said, I would elect to grant divine weaponry to mankind and aid their struggle. I do not like worlds in which people suffer heavily, after all." That made sense enough. I supposed that indirect intervention was also a fair option. It was enough to interfere, but also not be a massive boost. But then again, he said they wouldn't intervene in the natural order of the world, but they'd still grant some kind of superweapon to use in the case of big events like a Demon Lord uprising? It all sounded a little half-assed to me.

"There will always be those who depend on their parents forever. But the humans of this world are children no longer, I ask that you walk by yourselves, talk by yourselves. If you do so, you should be able to walk with pride and strength, to clear all obstacles in your path. With that, we Gods will watch over you keenly. Sometimes." That 'sometimes' was a little unnecessary. But I'm sure that someone was always being watched somewhere across all the universes, so it wasn't like they were slacking.

"B-But what am I to do…? If Lars, god of light, doesn't exist, then… All of his teachings were made by a man, rather than the divine. Does that make it all meaningless? Does that make all I've ever done completely meaningless?"

"It is not meaningless, far from it. I am certain that somewhere, at least once, those teachings have saved someone. It matters not who made them, so long as they do good. Simply look at it as 'for your fellow man' rather than 'for the glory of God.' Cast off the shackles of doctrine, and live by your own strengths."

"…Y-Yes…" I didn't think her mind would be able to change right away. After all, she had been born with a certain mindset, and raised in it. But, little by little, I felt she could be freed from the shackles she was born into.

"Well then, I believe it's time for me to leave. It is not proper for time to be put on pause for so long…" We moved back to my throne room, because it would've been strange if we suddenly vanished in front of everyone else.

Kohaku and Kousaka were both as stiff as they had been before. If it weren't for the unusual circumstances of the situation, I might've been inclined to pull a prank on them. It was a tad late for that, though.

"Well then, my dear. Live strong, live brave. Live in good health." God bore a beautiful smile, and turned into particles of light.

After a few moments, Kohaku and the others began to move again. They looked in our general direction, somewhat confused. Since my location was a little bit different to when time had stopped, I think it looked like I had teleported from their perspective.

"...I-It feels like I just woke from a dream. Did... did that really just happen?"

"It really did. You met with God, the one and only. Do you believe, now?"

"...I do." The girl wore a peaceful smile on her face, and the shine in her eyes seemed calmer, more serene. I hoped that she was able to reconcile things within herself.

Then, with a quick bow and an apology, she left my throne room.

So ended my first diplomatic meeting. I was immediately reprimanded by Kousaka. I couldn't really complain about that, though. I was not exactly good when it came to negotiation.

In all honesty I was a little concerned, so I dispatched one of Tsubaki's ninjas to the Theocracy. I summoned a tiny bird and asked him to take it along with him, so that I'd be able to know any news as soon as he got it.

A few days later, I learned that a priestess of the Ramissh Theocracy, one Phyllis Rugit, had been stripped of her position. She had been charged with high blasphemy, the penalty for which was death.

How could something so foolish have come about? I couldn't understand why Phyllis had been marked for execution. The world was too cruel a place, to allow this to happen to a girl who was finally able to act on her own thoughts.

《When is she to die?》

《Ah, yes… The execution is scheduled for three days from now, early in the morning. The only reason she wasn't cut down on the spot was because of the presence of a group that protested the order, and they didn't wish to create civil unrest.》 The agent I had sent to Ramissh was able to instantly report in through a telepathic link I had set up via a summoned bird familiar. From the sounds of things, Phyllis had some allies over there, so that was a small comfort to know. At the very least, I was glad she hadn't been killed yet.

《Thank you. Please continue your investigation, and let us know if there are any new major developments.》

《Very well.》 I cut off the contact. I had to figure out what to do. It was obvious from the outset that I couldn't leave her to die. I was the one responsible for Phyllis' new outlook on life, so the execution order was also my responsibility by proxy.

"Ugh… this is why religion is such a bore, Touya. Religious people are always convinced they're in the right, and never stop to consider other outlooks!" Elze, leaning her arms on the table at the balcony, failed to hide her irritation. I told everyone about the situation with Phyllis, though I took care to omit the part about us getting a visit from God. I just replaced that part by telling everyone that I had persuaded Phyllis to change her faith, or rather that she had left our meeting with a few things to reflect on and ponder.

"So, what will you do?"

"Well, I figured I'd go there. I have to stop the execution, right?" I gave Linze a simple enough answer. This was one of those situations where the fact that I was a head of state could come in handy. They couldn't just brush me off, surely. I decided that the best course of action was to directly negotiate with the pope. After all, the life of one former priest wouldn't be that difficult to negotiate sparing, right?

"And if they do not stop, if they do not, what will you do then?"

"Hm… it'll have to be a prison break, right? I'll bust in and save her."

"A-Are you stupid, Touya?! That'll cause an international incident!" Yumina didn't seem to like my response to Yae's question, but I decided to keep it as a last resort. I didn't think we needed to rely on Ramissh or anything, so if we ended up souring relations with them it wouldn't be the end of the world.

At first, I held back a little. I wasn't sure if Lars, god of light, was a real entity, and I didn't want to meddle in their religious affairs, but after God himself told me that Lars wasn't real? That changed everything. Ultimately, their religion was irrelevant to me in this matter, what mattered was their diplomatic attitude. Part of me wouldn't have even minded if diplomatic relations broke down between our two nations. They just sounded more like trouble than anything else to me.

I shifted my gaze to Kousaka, who was quietly standing nearby.

"Will there be any issues if I earn the ire of that country?"

"Currently, I see no major negative repercussions. But they may send their zealots to cause trouble in our country." Well that sounded a bit irritating. It struck me as odd that a God with teachings of light and justice would have such petulant, hounding followers.

"They can justify anything if they say it's in the name of justice… It's just a convenient excuse for them…" Lu let out a quiet mutter, disgust painted on her face. That reminded me of a saying I'd once heard. So long as everyone tries to be the hero, wars will never end.

"Anyway, I can't just abandon her like this. I'm off to go save her."

"Then at least let us come, too."

"No, if we all rush in at once it'll only needlessly agitate them. I'll take care of this one myself." Having said that, I decided to take Kohaku with me just to be safe. My decision must have seemed somewhat irresponsible for a head of state, but since we didn't know what to expect, I figured it'd be safest for me to handle it alone.

So long as everyone tries to be the hero, wars will never end.

"Oh, so you're the grand duke of Brunhild, are you? Sorry, kid, but I don't have time for your games right now. Go play royalty somewhere else." I made use of Babylon to go all the way to the capital of Ramissh, only to be turned away at the front door of the Isla Temple.

It was only to be expected, really. I had no real evidence to support my claim, after all. If some kid turned up out of nowhere and introduced himself as a monarch, I'd probably look at them funny, too.

"Look, can you just like, go fetch the pope for me or something? There's something important I need to talk to her about."

"*Fetch the pope…?!* Insolent brat! How dare you talk of our pope like she's some household pet!"

"Sorry? I don't believe in your religion, and I'm not even a citizen of your country. I don't see why you're getting worked up over something like that." I'd wanted to resolve things peacefully if possible, but the knight before me drew his sword in a fit of rage. *Whoa, this guy was quick to snap.* I nimbly dodged the knight's attack, following up with a chop to knock the sword out of his hands.

The metallic clang of the sword hitting the ground alerted the rest of the knights, who were swift to react as they poured out of the temple in droves.

"What happened?!"

"We've got an intruder! Some insolent brat calling himself the grand duke of Brunhild. He insulted the pope!"

"He did what?!" Two, four, six, eight… Around twenty knights in total. They had me surrounded before I could even react. They sure brought out a lot of people just to subdue one kid. For a group claiming to follow a god of light and justice, they sure didn't seem averse to using cowardly tactics. Though, when I thought about it, a team of heroes fighting together to defeat a single monster was actually fairly common in superhero shows. I decided to just stick these guys in that category for now. "I'll ask one more time. I, the grand duke of Brunhild, wish to meet with the Pope of Ramissh to discuss an important matter. Would anyone be kind enough to escort me to her?"

"We're not playing along with your little game, kid!" I brandished my weapon, and without hesitation fired a paralysis bullet at the first knight to charge at me. Seeing him collapse on the spot, the other knights faltered for a brief moment, but quickly pulled themselves together and raised a war cry.

Mithril in my right hand, Black Dragon horn in my left, I shot my way through the throng of knights with my trusty twin Brunhilds.

I immobilized their entire force in an instant. *That's what you get for not listening to me.*

"Truly a bothersome crowd, these people."

"You can say that again." I instinctively met Kohaku's analysis with a complaint of my own. Still, what was I to do from here? My options were to just continue like this and force my way in, or...

Deciding that this was a better course of action, I cast [Recovery] on one of the knights to undo the paralysis.

"There's a priest here called Nesto-what's-his-face, right? I want you to bring him to me. If he refuses, tell him I'll spill the secret about his head to everyone. That'll make him understand." I was already acquainted with that baldy priest, so I decided to seek him out first. He was more likely to hear me out than these guys were, at least.

The knight followed my instructions, taking off with a panicked dash into the temple. Before long, a group of what I could only call paladins came out of the temple fully clad in pure white armor, with Father Nesto leading the way. *Oh hey, he got a new wig.*

"Your Highness, the Grand Duke of Brunhild?! What brings you to this place?! No, before that, explain yourself! What is the meaning of this?!"

"I told the guard that I had important business with the pope. He refused to hear me out, and then a whole group of them attacked me without warning. I simply reacted in self-defense." So I explained, pointing at the listless knights littered on the ground.

"Do you understand your position here? You've shot down soldiers of a foreign country, and are attempting illegal entry into our sacred temple. This is an international incident!"

"And raising your sword against the ruler of a foreign country isn't? Nice double-standards you've got there." I could almost see the sparks flying as I met my eyes with Nesto's. What a pain. This guy clearly hated me. The feeling was mutual. *Whatever, I just need him to take me to the pope.*

"What is going on here?" This time it was a man wearing a gaudy robe who emerged from the temple. His hair was neatly swept-back, and he had a silly little mustache. He was the spitting image of a certain dictator. Ours would've been a little bit taller, though.

"Cardinal Zeon…?" Nesto turned his head and muttered. *Cardinal? If I remember right, aren't those like a few really important guys who work directly under the pope?*

"Father Nesto, who is this man? It is most unpleasant to have him causing a commotion on our sacred temple grounds." The cardinal clicked his tongue as he turned to face Father Nesto. *Oh boy, we've got a live one here.*

"He, he's… Err, I mean, this esteemed gentleman is His Highness the Grand Duke of Brunhild. He says that he wishes to meet with Her Holiness the Pope."

"This *boy* is…?!" The cardinal stared intently at me, looking me over as if appraising my worth. It made me realize something. When introducing myself as a leader, I should probably have been dressed the part. I made a mental note to ask Zanac to make me some kingly clothes next time I saw him. I honestly felt that too many people in the world judged others based on appearance alone.

"Your Highness the Grand Duke of Brunhild, was it?"

"That's me."

"What manner of business could a foreign ruler have with Her Eminence the Pope? If you'd like, I could relay a message to her on your behalf."

"Thank you, but I would much rather meet with Her Holiness in person. Could I trouble you to escort me to her, instead?" The cardinal and I clashed gazes with sly grins on our faces, each of us trying to sound the other out. I felt like I definitely couldn't trust this guy. If my plea to rescind Phyllis' execution were left in this guy's hands, I didn't think the pope would ever get to hear a thing about it.

"…Right this way." The cardinal invited me into the temple. I was led to a room and asked to wait there, with several paladins left behind to keep an eye on me. I sat obediently in a chair, keeping to myself as the paladins' gazes bored a hole in my back. I was neck-deep in unfamiliar territory.

They probably weren't stupid enough to assault me while we were inside the temple, but doing as I was told seemed like the best course of action for the time being.

After a short wait, the cardinal returned to the room.

"Her Eminence the Pope will see you now. Please, right this way." The cardinal led me around through several more corridors. The temple was unnecessarily huge. After climbing up a long staircase, we finally reached a fancy door with golden borders, beyond which was a large, spacious room.

Lined up by the left wall were several men in robes similar to the cardinal's, and to the right stood a row of paladins standing at attention. An elderly woman in pure white robes and a big, long hat sat with a sharp look on her face atop her raised platform. This lady was the popess, Elias Altra.

"Welcome to my temple, Grand Duke of Brunhild. I must admit to being rather startled by your abrupt visit, but as the pope, I have agreed to meet your request at an audience."

"A pleasure to make your acquaintance, Your Eminence. Please forgive my rudeness for barging in unannounced like this." I lowered my head as I spoke. I wasn't really at fault in the slightest, but I figured I should probably still apologize for beating up all their knights like that.

"...There is much I would like to say, but let us get straight to this business of yours. Whatever has brought you all this way to my temple?"

"Regarding the death sentence of one priest, Phyllis Rugit, I would request that the execution not be carried out." The entire hall was filled with mumbled whispers the moment that name left my lips. The pope took note of this, and shot me an intense look.

"What a farce this is. To think that a foreign leader would interfere in the death sentence of a convicted criminal... I cannot help but worry for the state of your kingdom."

"...A criminal, you say? Then tell me, what crime has she committed, exactly?"

"Her primary offense is her advocation that our God, Lars, is a figure of make-believe. This is an unforgivable sin for a priest to commit. In addition, she is suspected of being a vampire who has already attacked several people. A being of darkness with such an evil soul must be dealt with appropriately."

What? Phyllis is a vampire? What's that supposed to mean? Are they saying she hid that fact in order to become a priest and blend in?

《Master, do not let her mislead you. That girl was, without a doubt, an ordinary human being. I would be able to recognize a vampire by the smell alone.》 Kohaku supported me through telepathy. I knew I could count on Kohaku. But still, things were starting to look pretty suspicious. Almost as if the whole thing was one big, convenient set-up.

"That's strange. Shouldn't you be able to see through a vampire's disguise like that with your god's righteous powers?"

"...Lars will never allow evil to go unpunished. All who defy him shall meet with divine punishment. *Much like in this case.*" This wasn't "divine punishment" at all, it was just conveniently silencing dissenters. I began to suspect that this old lady already knew that Lars was a big old fraud.

"So you claim, but haven't there already been a number of victims? I feel that your god should have enacted his divine punishment *before* so many victims arose, don't you think?"

"Any such victims must have been carrying sins of their own. The truly devout would never have fallen prey to such evils." This was pointless. She was making baseless claims with that backward religious logic of hers.

"...Then I assume you have no intention of rescinding Phyllis' death sentence?"

"No evil can be allowed to go unpunished. Worry not, for we shall purify the girl's soul in the process. These very actions are naught but pure salvation for the girl." I let out a heavy sigh. The whole thing was just so stupid. *Non-believers are evil. When things go well, it's all thanks to God's guidance. When things aren't going well, it's because you don't have enough faith. And when a system based on these beliefs allows legal murder of innocent people, it just leaves me dumbstruck and appalled.*

"This is stupid. Every one of you here is truly beyond salvation."

"Wha...?!" My words froze the room into total silence. Even the pope stared at me wide-eyed. I was done playing along with these jokers. Since it didn't seem like words would be effective, I'd just do things my way instead.

"I'll declare it loudly for all to hear. Lars, the god of light, does not exist. He's a false idol, and Phyllis merely caught on to that fact. You're free to have your own beliefs, but stop labeling anyone who disagrees with them as evil. Don't think that being religious somehow automatically makes you better than everyone else."

"Silence! You will insult our God no further!" The paladins to my right all instantly moved their hands to the hilts of their swords.

"I'm very sorry about that. So sorry, in fact, that I'd like to apologize to Him in person. Bring your god Lars before me, and I'd happily kiss his feet." Not like they could, even if they wanted to.

"I reject the very notion of your god, and all that he stands for. I reject any teachings that could possibly allow one to enact false justice in the name of a false idol, dooming an innocent girl to an unjust death. I'll say it again. You have no God."

Their religion was unusual to begin with. Despite having been around for a thousand years, it remained mostly contained within their own country. Even considering that the magic of this world made it nigh-impossible to determine an actual "divine miracle," the fact that their religion had barely spread at all was plenty suspicious. If I were to use healing magic back in my own world, a new religion might spring up overnight. There would still be those who would call me a fraud, of course, but the fact would remain that I had healed a person's wounds, leading at least that person to believe in me. However, in this world the most you'd get is a few thanks; it definitely wouldn't be taken as a divine miracle. That was the nature of magic. That's just how things were over here.

They called it a religion, but living in this country you would naturally be surrounded and outnumbered by the devout everywhere you looked, leaving you with no choice but to follow suit. It wasn't about whether you really believed in the god or not; it looked more like a form of mind control in this case.

One important thing to note was that not a single country had formed an alliance with Ramissh. This country — or rather, the ground that the country rested on — might have been hiding something.

Taking Belfast as a comparison, the people there placed more faith in fairies than Gods. People who had met fairies could be found here and there, but nobody would claim to have met a God. According to the God that I knew, fairies were like the Gods' servants' servants or something.

At any rate, it was pointless to compare this religion to any of those from my old world. Heck, I still couldn't even be sure if this planet was round like Earth was.

Compared to the religions I knew, this one felt obviously different and horribly warped. It didn't seem like it was meant to lead people to salvation, or even just offer some peace of mind, at all. All I got from them was that they hated anyone who disagreed with them.

Coming to the country myself had only helped solidify that impression. There was clearly more to this country than it seemed.

"…And that's why I let myself get caught on purpose."

"I… see." I explained my plot to Kohaku as we sat together in an underground prison cell. *I swear I'm not just trying to save face.* After my outburst, I was one-sidedly labeled a villain. Naturally I'd be able to gather evidence after being caught. …That was definitely my plan, yeah.

"In that case… what do you intend to do now?"

"…Wh-What do you think I should do?" Kohaku leered at me, eyes filled with doubt. *I'm joking, it's a joke!*

"For now, Phyllis' safety comes first. After that, we'll gather info. Let's go."

The underground prison wasn't especially big, nor was it especially bright. It was sturdy, though. The stone walls surrounding us held firm. *Is this the kind of hospitality you want to give a neighboring monarch?!* I found it all a little bit excessive really. I wondered if they were going to just act like I was some miscreant who had pretended to be Brunhild's grand duke.

If that was the case, they might end up seriously trying to execute me. If someone from my country came to investigate, they could always cover it up and lie about me ever being here, too.

Welp, better break out already.

"[Mirage]." I created an illusory image of Kohaku and myself, and set it in a dingy prison corner. I didn't want them thinking we escaped, after all.

I considered using [Gate], but they'd placed down a barrier preventing that kind of magic. That stupid baldheaded priest probably tipped them off about it. But that was fine, there were other methods to escape, after all.

"Oh, right… better conceal ourselves…" I used [Invisible], a very convenient spell, to turn Kohaku and myself invisible. We could see one another, but nobody else could see us.

I then used [Modeling] to twist apart the bars of the prison and make my grand escape. Naturally I restored the bars to their original appearance after we got out, though.

I climbed up a tight stairway and found myself in a stone passage, lined with doors. At the other end, there were even more stairs going up. We were still in the underground section, so the guardsmen were still a bit ahead.

Each door was marked with a number, the one I had just exited was clearly cell number four.

"Map search. Phyllis Rugit."

"Understood. Search completed." My smartphone projected a small map and pointed out the location, it seemed to be cell number eight.

I closed my map. Even if my smartphone was concealed by my magic, the projected image it shot out was definitely visible. It'd be bad if somebody noticed that just floating around.

I opened up cell number eight and slowly descended the stairs into the dank underground.

After a while, the stairs were no more, and I saw Phyllis across on the other side of the dingy room. *Thank goodness, she's still alive... Doesn't look injured, either.*

I quickly noticed another person in the room, lying on the ground. She wasn't alone.

"Phyllis... Phyllis..." I didn't want to be too loud, so I gently called out to her. After a few moments, Phyllis slowly raised her head.

"...Wh-Who's there? Whose voice is that voice?" Phyllis began to look around, anxiety painted on her face. I had forgotten I was invisible.

I undid the spell, and revealed myself to her.

"Y-Your Highness the Grand Duke?!" I completely ignored her surprise and bent open the bars with my trusty spell. I turned to the side and slipped into the cell with her. *Wait a second, this jail's slightly larger than mine! Is this a form of discrimination? Am I being oppressed?*

"Why are you here of all places...?!"

"I came to help you, of course! I felt pretty responsible about that execution order!"

"N-No, Grand Duke, please! This isn't your doing, it's all mine...!"

"Shh, you're being too noisy!" I clamped a hand over Phyllis' mouth.

...... I-Is it okay? Maybe the guards'll just think she was talking to herself... I hope they don't get suspicious... Well, I don't hear anyone coming, at least...

"Phyllis, who's that sleeping person over there? Is she a friend?"

"That person... or rather... that woman... is Her Holiness the Pope, Elias Altra..."

"Excuse me?!" I suddenly blurted out my surprise, and instinctively covered my own mouth.

The goddamn pope of all people?! But wait, that can't be right... what about the old crone I met earlier with the piercing eyes?! This woman looked completely different. I took a closer peek at her face, and it was definitely not the same person. She was definitely about the same age, but this sleeping woman's face was far gentler and softer.

"Wait, this is Elias Altra?! Then who did I meet earlier?!"

"It's more likely that you met a different person entirely. Did she look similar age-wise, but with a more piercing gaze?"

"Yeah, kinda like that I guess."

"That was probably Cardinal Kyurei, then... She's Cardinal Zeon's elder sister." That would make her the sister of that annoying mustache guy. Hm, but that didn't add up... It seemed as though they'd prepared a fake pope and given me a fake audience with her! Which meant to me that they were all working together. This was beginning to seem like a seriously foul conspiracy.

"Sorry, I'm finding it a little hard to follow here... Can you tell me everything from the top?" According to Phyllis, after she returned home and reported to the pope and the others, everything went wrong. The cardinals were furious at her for the denial of their God, and the opposition of their doctrine. Immediately, they demanded she be executed. However, the pope herself, along with a few other priests, stood up and objected to that.

Phyllis wasn't entirely surprised by their reaction, but was amazed that the pope herself stood by her side. Regardless, she was arrested either way.

After a few days, the pope was also thrown into the dungeon, albeit in a severely weakened state.

"But why would they toss the pope of all people in prison…?"

"Th-That is because… the secret of this nation must be protected, at all costs." The pope opened up her eyes, and stared right at me. She seemed to have awoken. The pope's left eye was green, and her right eye was blue. Her eyes were heterochromatic, mismatched. It brought to mind Yumina's Mystic Eyes… "You are the grand duke of Brunhild, are you not…? My name is Elias Altra, it's a pleasure…" The pope herself slowly raised herself up and introduced herself. Despite her motions, however, she looked extremely weak. I decided she'd need to heal up.

I cast [**Recovery**] and [**Refresh**] on her, which brought her body back to relative strength. After that, I slapped on a [**Cure Heal**] for good measure.

As I healed her, I wondered why she hadn't just healed herself… but that was stupid, just because she worshiped a god of light didn't necessarily mean she'd have any talents with Light spells. I was pretty sure I remembered someone telling me Dark and Light were fairly rare attributes to have affinity for, anyway.

If it was similar to a fantasy RPG, then people who had healing magic would probably be priests who channeled the power of God through their spells. That kind of thing was a staple in videogames, but this was another world, not a game world. Even so, I couldn't help but think if that's how it worked, then the religion would've spread further and faster.

"Thank you so much for that... I feel considerably better."

"I'm glad. But more importantly, why were you brought here? You said something about this country's secret?"

"...... Hmh..."

She stayed quiet for a time, before looking right at me with a focused expression.

"It is a secret that would shake the very foundation of the country we stand in right now, but it seems there'd be no point in keeping it hidden from you. It is indeed as Phyllis said. Lars, god of light, does not exist." *What?* I was completely taken aback. The pope of a religion had just denied her own God. I looked a Phyllis, who seemed equally shocked.

"Each of the cardinals know the truth as well. After I ascended to cardinalhood before I was pope, the previous pope told me the truth as well." *That means the higher-ups knew... but they still continue the farce of believing in this Light God... why?* There was something more important than that, though. Sure, Phyllis and myself knew Lars didn't exist because God himself had verified that information for us. But how did the cardinals themselves know for sure that the God they worshiped wasn't real? "Long ago, this territory was the domain of monstrous beasts, demons, and wicked spirits. The one that appeared to purge these creatures was a man known as Ramirez. But Ramirez was not the priest our scriptures state he was."

"He wasn't...?" *Isn't Ramirez the founder of Ramissh? What's going on here?* "Ramirez was no priest, he was a mage. One that specialized in summoning. His greatest affinity was Dark magic."

"What...?!"

126

"The scriptures state that Ramirez summoned Lars, god of light, to purge the land of wickedness. But the truth is different entirely. What Ramirez called down were wicked spirits, servants of the darkness. After he used that power to purge the land of beasts, he came up with an idea, and began to set it into motion." *Hm, so God was right after all, he'd summoned powerful spirits. But they weren't light, they were creatures of the dark... Still, Ramirez must've been a hell of a guy to call upon dark stuff like that...* My attention turned back to Elias, who was explaining what the man's idea was. "Ramirez thought he would build a kingdom upon his newly-conquered land, using the powers of dark spirits to manipulate the minds of the people who lived there. That's how he began the Lars faith. The dark spirits he summoned merged into one great beast, and meddled with the minds of the people who were brought into the area. Through this method, their thoughts were twisted in line with Ramirez's. All of the citizens accepted Ramirez's doctrine without question, and the Ramissh Theocracy was formally founded." *What the hell...?! Isn't that just brainwashing?! Or maybe it could be called something more akin to hypnosis... still, twisting people's brains like that? That's totally messed up.*

"Was the Dark Spirit's mental conditioning that strong?"

"The influence of the spirit made it easier for him to convince people of his ideals, but people who were resistant to magic ended up being less affected by it. That's why Lars, god of light was created as a figurehead for the faith. He used mental conditioning, and an idol people could aspire to. Using that wicked combination, he captured both the hearts and the minds of his people." Ramirez disgusted me. I wasn't surprised that they were so desperate to keep the secret. Their entire religion would collapse if this leaked out. It was truly heinous that a religion built on the ideals of light was actually spawned by a monster from the dark…

"…I understand that this is a really important secret, but… Why does this mean the pope had to be locked up?"

"I protected Phyllis, so they believed I may have gone rogue and threatened to spill the truth. Not to mention the fact that both Kyurei and Zeon were originally in the running for popehood, and saw an opportunity to supplant me and my position. I was gradually fed a medication that poisoned my body and weakened my mind. They didn't have to kill me to replace me, after all." That made sense enough. They probably had no idea why I'd come to their country, and with the pope being absent they decided to trick me into a fake meeting… They were probably suspicious because of what had happened with Phyllis, too… They didn't handle it very well, though.

"But, Your Holiness… why did you protect Phyllis? Aren't you kind of meant to be the figurehead of the religion? Why would you stand by someone who would shake the faith so much?" I didn't get it at all. If I were a pope, then someone like Phyllis would be seen as a pest.

"…I truly believed in Lars, god of light… it's why I joined the priesthood. I worked hard, for the sake of my Lord. But when I became a cardinal… They told me there was no God. That my work was fruitless. After that, I simply worked to maintain the lie, a cog in the wheel like all the rest. Once you learn the truth, there's no going back to normality." That sounded pretty rough to me. I figured they'd probably set up methods to silence anyone that threatened to reveal the truth anyway. Dead men tell no tales, after all. And now I had learned this secret, so they'd probably end up after my head if I wasn't careful.

"Before I knew it, I had ascended to the position of pope. But it was an empty position, my heart was already withered. I was trapped in a place that I couldn't possibly abandon. Then, Phyllis came and told us what she had seen. She appeared, truly convinced that there was indeed a God out there." After speaking, the pope turned to Phyllis. She turned to me, vigor in her voice, a beautiful smile painting her face.

"Can you imagine the euphoria I felt in that moment? It was indeed true that Lars, god of light, did not exist, but... there *was* in fact a God that did exist. And there was a person who had actually met Him! The words that she had heard from God, I was desperate to learn more. It was the first time in years that my heart truly began beating again."

"But why did you believe Phyllis without question? You didn't doubt her at all?" After I asked, the pope pointed to her left eye. Her pale green eye suddenly turned darker.

"I possess the Mystic Eyes of Sincerity. I've never been able to miss a lie. It was also one of the reasons I was elected as pope. When Phyllis told me her story, I knew she was no liar. I learned in that moment that God truly existed, and it made me so happy. In that moment, I was euphoric, because of God's blessing. I was also envious, as I wished to meet God myself..." The pope let out a quiet, sad mutter. *Oh. Oh no.* Before I could stop it, I realized what was about to happen. I turned to look at Kohaku. The tiger was frozen stiff!

"Yoo-hoo! Did someone want to meet little old me?"

From the darkness, God himself descended, clad in dazzling light.

God, please! You're way too whimsical!

"Have you just been watching this whole time?"

"It had been weighing on my mind. The poor girl had been locked away because I had done something I shouldn't have, and I felt rather guilty about it all. But then, as God, I couldn't exactly come to her rescue myself…" I knew what he meant. The root cause of all that was going on could be narrowed down to carelessness on God's part.

I stole a glance in Phyllis' direction and noticed that she'd already fallen prostrate before His divine presence, while the pope stood, mouth slack, staring at us in confusion.

"Umm… Your Highness, who might this be?"

"This is God."

"G-G-God…?!" The pope's eyes snapped wide open, and she gazed at both God and I in turn. She was certainly surprised, but it seemed she still had some doubts. I could feel her using her Mystic Eyes on me. She could tell that I wasn't lying, but it seemed like she hadn't quite fully grasped the reality of the situation yet.

"Oh, I know. God, do that flashy halo thing you did before."

"Eh? I thought you told me not to use my divine aura anymore."

"You have my permission this time." God nodded and gradually begin to let out his divine aura. *Welp, here it comes.*

God's majestic form lit up for all to behold. His halo of divinity was as impressive as ever. One glance would be enough to convince anyone that this person was, indeed, the one true God.

Bathed in His divine light, the pope also laid herself prostrate on the ground next to Phyllis.

"Can I turn it off now?"

"Yup, that'll do." The imposing light vanished as swiftly as it came. Just then, a certain doubt floated up from the back of my mind. Why was it that I could resist his divine aura which should easily have overwhelmed any normal human? Was that another one of the perks he gave me when I was sent to this world?

"Is there something the matter?"

"Hm? Oh, I was just wondering why your aura doesn't completely overwhelm me like it seems to do to everyone else. I just figured maybe you'd done something that would give me some resistance to it." God looked at the two girls at his feet and tilted his head.

"...Come to think of it, that is rather strange. Any ordinary — or even extraordinary — human being exposed to my divine presence in its true form should be left bowing before me in awe, like these two girls. None of my gifts to you included a resistance to Divinity itself, so I cannot think what would be... Ohh!"

"...God, what did you do to me?" *What's with that face?! Why do you look like you're screaming "Oh, shit!" in your head?! Looking away is just making you look more suspicious! And why are you trying to play it off by whistling? These days not even cartoon characters do that!*

"...You're a poor liar, God."

"Erm... Weeell... Could you wait for just one moment?" He raised his right arm aloft and unleashed some kind of power. I couldn't tell what he'd done for a moment.

"I've stopped time for the girls, as well. It would be rather troublesome if anyone were to ever learn of this, you see." The girls had already been paralyzed in their positions bowing before God's feet anyway, so it didn't really feel any different from a moment ago. Still, if God said so…

"Well? Out with it."

"Hrmm… To summarize, you have already died once, back in your old world. I took responsibility for that and reincarnated you, but…"

"But?" I couldn't see what he was getting at. Heck, I was actually pretty thankful to him for giving me a new life in this world.

"Normally when reviving someone, I would repair the damage done to their physical or spiritual body using the basic elements and energy of that specific world. In your case, though, I summoned you straight up to the Divine Realm before anything else. Physical body and all. Only *after* that did I revive you into a new world."

"I'm afraid I don't follow."

"Well, I revived you using the materials I had at hand. And since your body and soul were both in the Divine Realm at the time, I ended up putting you back together with divine matter. To put it simply, your body is similar in composition to that of a God." This was the first I'd heard any of this. I was dumbstruck.

"B-But I still get exhausted if I run for too long, and I can still get injured like anyone else. It doesn't really *feel* like I've got a God's body…"

"Well, it *has* only been one year since you were reincarnated, your powers might not have fully bloomed yet. Can you think of any similar situations where your strengths or resistances have felt rather abnormal for a human being?" … More than I could count. My near-limitless mana pool, and my ability to use any Null spell I wanted, for example. I'd always chalked it up to being "God's gift," but… It turned out that it was actually "all God's *fault*."

"My mistake. Wahahaaah!"

"Don't just laugh it off like that... Please tell me there aren't going to be any adverse effects to this later on down the line."

"None at all. Think of it as just having obtained a much sturdier body than the norm. Although, you may find yourself awakening to some strange new powers later on... if I'm right, your body is like that of an infant God's right now. So please let me know if something like that does happen." *Whaddya mean by strange new powers?! I damn sure hope that I won't randomly wake up one day with a halo of divinity radiating from my entire body...*

... I decided not to worry about it. If it wasn't gonna kill me or directly harm me in any way, then I figured I could live with it. Just so long as I could continue living out my life in this world, that was enough for me.

Just then, something came to mind that might've been able to destroy my peaceful life in this world.

"Hey, God, do you know anything about the Phrase?"

"Phrase? Nothing comes to mind, I am afraid to say." I figured as much. I seemed to recall him saying that he hadn't been checking in on this world much until after he sent me here. As God would say, if a world faced potential destruction, then it was up to that world's inhabitants to find a solution to that which didn't involve divine intervention.

But if God wasn't the one who drove the Phrase away around five thousand years prior, that only made me question what caused them to leave...

His explanation finished, God raised his hand once more and let out that same power as before. I assumed the girls could now move again, but it was hard to tell since they were still bowing before God as they had been this whole time. Kohaku, however, was quite clearly still frozen in time. I felt kind of bad for Kohaku being the only one left out…

"You can stand up now. I'm very sorry that my carelessness has put you in this difficult situation, young lady."

"N-Not at all! P-P-P-Please, think nothing of it!"

"It seems as though I've even managed to get the pope wrapped up in it… I'm truly sorry about all this."

"Th-thank—… I am grateful for your words…" The two finally raised their heads. This was Phyllis' second time meeting God, so although she was nervous, she could at least look him in the face. On the other hand, the pope had just exchanged words with God himself, and the encounter had left her with tears flowing down her face. Well, it *was* a pretty life-changing experience for her, to put it lightly.

"I overheard your conversation. It must have pained you greatly to have lived your whole life embracing a lie like that. Fret not, though. All will be fine now."

"Such benevolence…!"

"Whaddya mean, everything's gonna be fine? Are you gonna step in and resolve the whole situation for us?" For a moment I was worried that he planned to just walk out in front of everyone with his halo on full power and declare "Your god of light doesn't exist. There, religion disproved," and wrap it all up with a clap of his hands. I mean, that *did* seem like the quickest and easiest solution, but…

"Not me, Touya my boy, *you* are. After all, that's what you've always done until now, is it not?" This irresponsible God was just planning on making me clean up after his mess! I couldn't believe his audacity. I knew I wasn't supposed to rely on divine intervention to solve my problems, but still!

"Uhm… taking the cardinals out of the picture wouldn't work out so well. If the truth were exposed, then there'd be public outcry." But really it was more likely that we'd just be branded as liars. After all, who would believe us?

"It is not as if the citizens are at fault, but… As things stand, they would only continue to believe in their god of light. There's nothing inherently wrong with that, but their justification of anything under the banner of light and justice cannot be excused."

"I don't believe this country can continue to function if we simply outed God as fake… If only there were some way to maintain the charade, but change the teachings…" The pope let out a saddened mutter.

It certainly wasn't a simple thing to change the foundation of a religion. It's not like you could just toss half a bible out the window and call it a day. I had no idea how to deal with that…

Hm, maybe some kind of incident could change how things are seen around here… Maybe God could just show up, and… no, that'd be too much interference. Guess we're on our own.

"Well, I will leave it to Touya. Now, that matter aside… Shouldn't we deal with the fellow beneath us?" God tapped on the stone floor with his foot, smiling gently. *Beneath us? What do you mean?* I turned to the pope, whose expression had quickly turned grave.

"Y-You noticed it…? Th-The presence down there is the Dark Spirit that Ramirez summoned… it's been beneath the temple since the inception of the Theocracy…"

"It what?!" *Wait, that monster's been lurking down there for the last thousand years?! Spirit or not, wasn't it summoned?! I thought summoned creatures needed magic energy to stick around!! Wait no, more importantly, why is it still here?!*

"It didn't take long for Ramirez to found the Ramissh Theocracy with the Dark Spirit's aid, but… shortly afterward, his mind was completely eroded and the man's mind was taken over by the beast. After all of that, the spirit fused with Ramirez's body and the cardinals of the era sealed it beneath the temple grounds. It was better for them to keep it here, actually… Because the Dark Spirit's ability of mentally conditioning everyone in the area never wore off. The brainwashing ability still emanates from it even to this day. Undying, but no longer alive, you could say Ramirez still supports the religion even in this state now." The pope spoke directly to God, as if confessing a grave sin.

That was a hell of a story. If that was true, it meant that such a horrible secret had been passed from cardinal to cardinal for the last thousand years. I finally understood how insidious this religion truly was. It also explained how the Dark Spirit was still here. If it fused with the summoner and sustained his body, then it could live here indefinitely. Though, I doubted he was still conscious after so long.

"The magical power of the Dark Spirit cannot affect you, or this girl, on account of your high magic resistances… but that does not apply to the regular folk here. Even now, they are being unconsciously influenced by Ramirez and his original doctrine."

"So that means, if we can deal with the spirit…"

"Correct, my boy. The zealous faith will disappear from the hearts and minds of the people. From then on, it would depend on the true feelings of the individual." That made sense. We had to kill it at the source. But I still had the feeling there'd be some rotten types who'd do anything under the banner of their own justice, even if we broke the mental interference.

"But I would suggest you two make haste. You said they sealed him, yes? I am quite sure that the seal is weaker than ever right now, and darkness is already emanating from its lair."

"You're right... In fact, there's been a string of people losing their energy, and even their lives... We officially blamed that on the work of a vampire, but in truth... it was because the spirit seal is waning." Well, that explained the vampire plot thread away quite nicely. Still, it was pretty bad if it was starting to drain people's lives. It made me wonder if the Dark Spirit was trying to build power or something...

"We need to deal with this Dark Spirit before it's too late... Your Eminence, do you have anyone in this country that would side with you if it came to it?"

"There are a few amongst the clergy that hope for the same outcome as I. But our numbers are minute compared to those backing Cardinal Zeon." It was better than nobody, at least. I wanted to avoid revealing the true origins of the country to the public, though, and everything about the Dark Spirit's mind control. But, I also wanted the cruel and inconvenient justice that Lars, god of light's doctrine spoke of to be stricken out entirely.

"Very well, I think I have seen enough. I will keep watching from my perch, so best of luck, Touya my boy! See you soon!"

"What?! Wait!! You can't jus—!" Before I could voice my protests, God vanished into beams of light. *You coward! Get back here!! You're making me deal with these messes that aren't even mine, augh!!* But, as much as I didn't want it to, time began to flow again. Kohaku eyed me with suspicion.

《My liege. I feel as though something very unusual just happened to you...》

《Don't mind it. It's no threat to us.》

《Very well…》 From Kohaku's perspective, we must've instantly teleported from one position to another, so the tiger was having difficulty processing how our pose and location had shifted so suddenly. It would be a pain to explain though, so I decided not to bother.

"…I feel as though I've awakened from a dream."

"Me too, Your Holiness…" I wondered if that was part of the exhilaration of meeting with God. As I watched the pope and Phyllis giggling together, something bit at my mind.

I felt it, an unpleasant crawling sensation up my spine. An electric shock that jolted right through me, making me feel ill. *It… can't be…*

"…Don't panic now, but… The Dark Spirit's seal just broke."

"Wh-What?!" Phyllis went pale in the face. Then, we heard the rumbling from below. It got louder, and louder. *We need to get out, now!* I twisted the iron bars with [**Modeling**] and carted Phyllis and the pope along with me up the stairs. The rumbling grew steadier, faster, louder. I had no doubts that the earth beneath us would crumble in seconds. We came out into the long passageway that led into other cells, and I quickly checked for other prisoners. Thankfully there were none, so we continued upward.

"Prisoners?! How did you escape from your cel— haghgh!!" We passed a guard, and I instinctively shot a paralysis bullet at him. *Ah crap… I can't leave him here, can I?!* "Kohaku, return to your beast form!"

"As you wish!" The pope opened her eyes wide in surprise as Kohaku both spoke, and turned into an enormous White Tiger. But I had no time to explain, I simply put the knocked-out guard on Kohaku's back, and continued running.

As we escaped from the prison, we came out into the temple's halls. I continued to run, finally stopping in a courtyard. It was at this point that I realized it was no longer day time. The moon was high in the sky. I checked the time, and it was just past the stroke of midnight.

The barrier wasn't set up across the entire temple, so I used [Gate] to take us to the middle of town.

The rumbling beneath the ground became more of a violent quake. Unsurprisingly, the streets were filled with bewildered people, apparently they assumed it was a simple earthquake scare. They didn't seem extremely afraid, so I figured earthquakes weren't uncommon in this region.

As I took the guardsman off Kohaku's back, the people in the area quickly noticed I was with Her Eminence the Pope. That wasn't especially surprising, she was the head of their state and seemed quite well-known. Everyone in the streets began swarming around her. They were probably uneasy, because the rumbling wasn't getting any gentler.

"Y-Your Eminence! What is going on?!"

"Please, everyone! Be calm! For your own safety, you must vacate the—" Just as she began telling the people to take refuge, an enormous explosion blasted away part of the temple. From amidst the dust and debris, something began crawling out of the building. *WHAT THE ACTUAL HELL IS THAT THING?!* It was enormous. Its shape wasn't even remotely human. Its skin was pitch, two black horns jutted from its head. On its side, countless grasping arms writhed from its body. On its back, six long tentacles squirmed. Its lower body was a mass of tendrils, without number. And its head had no eyes, only an enormous mouth, one that almost split across its entire face.

139

"GauUguguHGhh!! GooOoraaRaaAagGghH!!" It raised a monstrous roar, as if the depths of the earth were screaming for salvation.

The air itself trembled. The sound it released was enough to bring the townspeople to their knees with fear. The ground began to tremble, people everywhere dropped to the ground. *Is it manipulating people's minds? Making them afraid?!*

This thing's like... a god of evil... I couldn't stop that cliche kind of term from floating up into my head. This was the Dark Spirit that was once called forth and manipulated by the summoner known as Ramirez. But now, it was in command. And after a thousand years... it was free.

I can't stress enough how big this thing was. Its dark tendrils moved forward, and the creature began to rise up. It was enormous, and ominous enough to strike disgust into the hearts of anyone.

One of its back-tentacles came down, smashing apart some of the temple. It let out another scream as debris and dust scattered around the area. This thing was a serious threat.

"GoGOaghaAgGuU!!" Unintelligible nonsense leaked from its maw, which was now unhinged and wide open. Along with the sound, a tar-like black fluid began bubbling out of its mouth like vomit.

Droplets of the stuff began falling, but they didn't hit the ground. Before they had a chance to, they transformed into winged, bat-like creatures. They had insectoid legs, but muscular human torsos. Their heads were elongated, but had no defined features like eyes, noses, or ears. Just mouths.

They flapped their wings and scattered across the city. The townsfolk began to shriek and scream, the entire city became a discordant tune of horror.

"GaAaAhgUGuhhRuuUugghahaAahahaAaA!!" The Dark Spirit screamed toward the heavens.

"I-It's a monster!"

"G-God will... God will s-surely save us... y-yeah...!" All around me, I heard people lapse into desperate prayer. *Sorry, but this monster... is your god.*

It probably didn't even remember Ramirez at this point. I could only assume that the spirit was operating on some base, destructive impulse.

"You said a thousand years ago that the cardinals teamed up to seal it away, right? Can't we do that again?!"

"I don't think we can... We simply can't match up to the power of the church from back then. The majority of the appointed cardinals nowadays can't even use magic!" *That's useless, then... Well, I guess what she says makes sense. If we were to compare the two eras, the difference is clear. In the olden days they probably prioritized strength or wisdom, but the current clergymen are just people in it for the faith, or political gain. Which makes them completely useless when the going actually gets tough.*

Guess there's nothing for it... But what can I... oh... there's an idea.

A sudden flash of inspiration struck my mind.

To be blunt, I saw an opportunity to change their doctrine at its core. Obviously having the real God appear was a no-no, but that didn't mean I couldn't pretend to be him. If I did that, defeated the monster, gave the pope some kind of fake divine message, and said a few words... then she'd definitely have the upper hand against the cardinals, and I could quash the idea of Lars once and for all!

But wait... isn't this just as dishonest as Ramirez? I am tricking everyone... But, hm... even if I am tricking everyone, I'm tricking

141

everyone with the best intentions! I'm just going along with what the actual God wants, acting on his behalf, so it's fine... right? I wasn't able to decide by myself, so I quickly took the pope and Phyllis aside and asked them about it.

"...If I'm entirely honest, I do not wish to deceive my people. But, I think we could create a much better situation than we've ever had before. If we defeat this beast, then we at least stop it from influencing their minds. That way, the warped ideals of justice can be easily removed from our doctrine as well." Her Holiness looked right at me, and asserted her belief. She had no hesitation.

"As pope, I have spread the gospel of a God I knew did not exist. I was crushed by guilt, restraining my true feelings and refusing to show them. I told myself it was for the sake of the Theocracy, but... If we were to change the doctrine, I would freely talk of God. The God you spoke of, Grand Duke, He would be the God I speak of. Even if the people don't know it, I would carry His ideals in my heart, proudly puff out my chest, and be happy. Don't you think such a thing would be wonderful?" I agreed. Though I felt a little awkward for using God's name in vain like this... it was still necessary.

After all, I was sure the citizens would be happier if the monster threatening them was slain by their God, and not by the leader of a foreign nation. And, on an international level, this would definitely give Brunhild a more favorable position with the bigwigs of Ramissh. ... That being said, I wasn't motivated by such things.

"B-But will you really be okay?! Can you win against such a huge beast?! It's the Dark Spirit, understand?!"

"Mmm... I think I can handle it." Phyllis had reasonable concerns, but I had an inkling that it wouldn't be as tough as I expected.

This spirit's specialty was likely its brainwashing ability. And, from what I understood, it was an area-of-effect skill rather than a direct target kind of thing. In short, it worked in a large area, which is probably why Ramirez thought to use it to govern a nation.

For someone like me, with my obscene magical resistance, it was no matter of concern. That being said, I didn't want to hang around it for too long... I had a feeling I couldn't resist it forever. In fact, it was pretty much a guarantee. Even Ramirez fell victim.

I think I'll be fine, but I won't know until I give it a go... The only issue now is making myself look like a God. I decided that the best way to handle it would be to cast [**Mirage**] on myself and call it a day.

As I headed toward it, the Dark Spirit cracked one of its tentacles across the ground, shattering streets and houses. It seemed to deal basic physical attacks, which definitely weren't a matter of concern for me.

I should probably hurry, though... the entire Holy Capital is gonna go up in rubble if I don't. I left the pope, Phyllis, and the townsfolk, and hid in a back alley. The two girls were leading a prayer circle. Typically I'd have told them to leave, but this was part of the plan. I would descend, as God, in response to their prayers.

I changed my appearance with my [**Mirage**] spell. Although it was more like I was masking myself than actually transforming. I decided to take the form of a traditional Greek-style God with long flowing blond hair, and blue eyes. I made myself pretty handsome, too.

"Well?"

"It looks good, but it feels like something's missing..." Kohaku gave the tiger equivalent of a shrug. *But I look just about as plain as the real God! It's not my fault you haven't met him! What kind of Heavenly Beast are you if you haven't even met God, huh?!*

Hm… what's missing then… how about… I created another illusion that caused light to cloak my entire body. I briefly considered adding a halo and angel wings, but I didn't want to look like an angel. If I ended up being a messenger from God, rather than God himself, that would defeat the point.

Just as I was putting the last parts of my disguise together, I realized something. Normally people would expect a God to actually fly in the sky, descending from the heavens. If I just appeared and walked amongst people, claiming to be God… that'd be a little weird. I really should've learned a flight spell. I made a mental note to pick one up later. *Ugh, pretending to be God is a real pain in the ass, I hate this!* Still, there was nothing I could do about it. I decided to project the image of God into the sky… Which completely defeated the point of cladding myself in it to begin with! *Then again, I'm going to have to look like this when I fight the monster anyway, so I guess it's fine.*

As I projected the divine image of the one true God into the sky above the city, the people let out yell of wonder and surprise. God had descended, and He was basking them in His glow. *First thing's first, we've gotta take care of those minions.*

"Come forth, Dark! I Seek the Shining Warmaiden: [Valkyrie]!" …Frankly, calling forth divine warriors to help me with a chant of "Come forth, Dark" sounded super silly to me, but I had to roll with the punches.

Summoning circles appeared around the projected God illusion, and angelic warmaidens were called forth into the sky. I made a contract with Valkyries after the incident in the Regulus Empire. I liked the Griffins, but having them as my sole air support was troublesome.

《The Dark Spirit has created shadowy monsters, slay them, and protect the townspeople.》 I conveyed telepathic orders to the angelic maidens, and they scattered across the city.

It honestly would've been easier to use my smartphone to lock on to all of them and wipe them out at once with Light magic, but they would've died too quickly. The citizens wouldn't have even known what saved them, and that wouldn't do. I was directing a scenario here!

Still, people's lives were at stake. I didn't think the Dark Spirit's minions were specifically targeting people, they seemed more like they were mindlessly rampaging, but that didn't mean they were any less dangerous. If they continued roaming around and trashing whatever, then people could still die through collateral damage.

The townspeople began to cheer, which was only natural. God himself and a band of angels had just appeared to fight their enemy.

Alrighty, time to move. I made myself disappear with **[Invisible],** and dashed across the rooftops, making sure to keep an eye on the God illusion I had projected up into the sky.

Man, at times like this I could really use a flight spell... Wonder if it's wind magic... or maybe it's a Null spell? Yeah, if it was Wind then Leen would be able to use it easily... It's gotta be a Null one.

I finally arrived before the temple, and got a real sense of how big the Dark Spirit was.

I erased the illusion of God in the sky, and, while maintaining the illusion of God on my own body, took out a two-meter-long sword from my storage.

I'd reduced the weight of the blade using **[Gravity]** so I could wield it in one hand, and it was created from a Phrase fragment. The material the blade was made of kind of made the surface sparkle and

145

dance with light, like the surface of water. I decided it was sufficiently mystical enough to pass off as a Godly weapon.

The Dark Spirit turned and glared down at me. Well, I said glared, but it had no eyes. Sure felt like a glare, though. A few of its back-tentacles whipped toward me.

"Hup…!" I jumped to the side and made a horizontal swing of the sword. I cleanly cut the tentacle, and the dark mass fell to the ground. A foul black fog began leaking from the sliced-off tentacle. …*Gross.*

But I didn't have any time to react before the tentacle vanished, and a new one took its place on the monster's body. *Wait, this thing can regenerate as well? That's irritating!*

As a (fake) God, I couldn't let anyone see it give me a hard time, so I needed to kill it fast. I briefly considered using [**Slip**], but it was so big that it'd definitely destroy a chunk of the city if it fell over. *Maybe I should crush it!*

"Target lock. The Dark Spirit. Invoke [**Gravity**]."

"Acknowledged. Target acquired. Invoking [**Gravity**]." The Dark Spirit immediately began to fall, it couldn't support its new, increased body weight. With a scream, it fell on to its side.

The area of the city beneath it was, naturally, completely leveled. *Ah crap! I pretty much got the same result I would've if I'd used* [**Slip**]! *Welp. God did it, not me.* At the very least, the people in the immediate area should've evacuated by that point, so nobody would get harmed.

This is pretty bad though. I think I may have overdone it with the flashiness…

There was nothing I could do, so I focused on wiping it out with an overwhelming show of force. I amplified the effects of [**Gravity**] on the creature, but couldn't be sure if I'd even changed much. It didn't have a face, so I couldn't gauge how it was feeling, either. Regardless, it seemed that I had it pinned down. *Now, for the finale!*

"Strike true, Light! Sparkling Holy Lance: [Shining Javelin]!" The spears of light drilled their way through the beast's body, and... The holes left in the creature didn't regenerate. It stood to reason that a Dark Spirit would be weak to Light magic.

"Target Lock. Launch an additional... one hundred... no, two hundred **[Shining Javelin]** strikes at the Dark Spirit!"

"Acknowledged. Target acquired." It was time for this monster to get a taste of (fake) God's (two-hundred-javelins of) wrath!

"Fire!"

"Acknowledged. Launching attack."

BOOM, CRASH, RUMBLE, SHAKOOM, BADABOOM!!!

The ground began to shake, which was natural, those Shining Javelins were really doing a number on the thing. The Dark Spirit's body split repeatedly, fragmenting as each new blade of light fell down upon it. As the volley ended, there was little left of the creature itself.

The fragmented pieces of the spirit spread across the area like a blackened fog. I figured that it was probably still alive, in some base form. I couldn't have that, though, it'd be a real pain if it resurrected or something. Therefore, I decided to annihilate it entirely.

"Come forth, Light. Shining Exile: [Banish]!" I cast a purifying spell over a large radius, scattering light everywhere. The wicked fog quickly scattered and dissipated.

As the light faded and the darkness of the spirit swirled into nothingness, a single skeleton clattered to the ground. In an instant, it crumbled to dust and blew away in the breeze...

I wondered if that was Ramirez. After a thousand years, he was finally freed. I honestly felt a little pity, but he fell victim to his own misdeeds in the end.

Alright, now was the time... I had to work hard and deceive everyone.

I looked across the streets as cheers resounded from every corner. Even amidst the dark of the night, I could hear people far and wide.

"Amazing! He did it!"

"Lars, thank you o Lars! The god of light has vanquished the wicked one!"

"Take that, you monster! Feel the wrath of our lord, you fiend!" The citizens cheered and jeered with enthusiasm, but I was just left feeling irritated.

I didn't know if it was just due to the residual brainwashing, but they were yammering on about Lars. I decided I'd show them the wrath of God they were cheering so much.

It seemed a feat wouldn't have been enough, so I had to preach to them directly.

"Target Lock. Effective range, within the city's borders. Invoke [**Lightning Javelin**] in random locations, ensuring that there are no people within ten meters of the spell. Repeat three hundred times."

"Understood. Target acquired. Invoking [**Lightning Javelin**]." All of a sudden, three hundred bolts fell from the sky and struck the city. Screams and shrieks broke out, and the townsfolk were sent into disarray.

I used my smartphone to project my image high into the sky, ensuring it could be seen at a distance.

"Do not speak so carelessly of justice, wrath, and indignation. It was the warped justice of your people that created this beast to begin with!" Then I decided to spice things up a bit. Using a [Gate], I brought the pope to my location. Her image too, was projected into the sky, and the citizens cheered in admiration. I gave the pope a knowing nod, and she knelt before me, bowing her head.

"Is it you, Your Divinity? Lars, god of light?"

"I am not, my child. I am indeed god's light, but I bear not the name of Lars. There is no such god named Lars." The people watching broke out into confusion again. That was natural, though. I'd just denied their god through-and-through.

"Step forth, young one. I've a message for you all." I placed my hand on the pope's forehead, and a dazzling light engulfed us both. I was a little tired by the charade, and tried to speed it up a bit. It's not like I had actually imbued a message into her mind, it was just dramatic effect.

After the light faded, the pope fully prostrated herself before me. Frankly I thought it was a little bit of overkill on her part.

Either way, I simply moved on to the next part.

"One final matter. I must bestow divine punishment upon those who accumulated sin, and allowed many crimes to be committed under the fraudulent guise of justice and light." I used my portal once again in a similar fashion to bring forth the assholes who had shown themselves to me earlier on. Cardinal Zeon, his sister Kyurei, the other cardinals, and the Templars who had hassled me all bowed before my divine might.

"Confess your sins to me."

"W-We've committed no crime, indulged in no sin! I-I'm a devout follower of your radiance, the light of God is my shepherd, I p-p-promise!!" Zeon began blabbering like an idiot, his face mashing into the ground in reverence. I couldn't believe he'd even try to worm his way out of the situation in front of God. It didn't matter that I was pretending, he didn't know that! This guy really was an idiot if he thought he could fool the divine.

"You miserable whelp. Claiming an innocent girl to be a vampire, going so far as to plan her death… Confining your very pope to a dingy jail cell?! You thought such things would escape my omnipotent gaze?!"

"Th-That was just…!!" Both Zeon and his sister went pale. The citizens, who were still looking on, began murmuring amongst themselves. The cardinals, the Templars, and everyone else present couldn't seem to contain their shock and horror.

"And you know as well as I that they were not your only crimes. Shall I disclose your other transgressions? One by one?!"

"N-Ngh…!" Zeon fell silent. I had asked the perfect leading question. I had no doubt in my mind that he had done all manner of terrible things under the banner of God, but I wasn't entirely certain of what they were. But now I knew he and his sister were beyond salvation.

Even while knowing there was no god of light, the two of them still conveniently used the image for their own ends. I couldn't afford to let them off the hook.

"Repent, mongrels!"

"Ughaah!!" I used my trusty paralyzing spell on everyone before me, except the pope of course. I then turned to Her Eminence, and spoke thus.

"I entrust their punishment to you, my child."

"Of course."

"Light and Dark are two sides of the same coin, forever indivisible. Justice, injustice, both are creations of human hands. If you commit to one side, you will ultimately tip into the other. Do not allow this." I faced the citizens and made my final declaration. That being said, I don't really think I made a very good speech. I decided to bail before I slipped up any more and got caught out.

I had the Valkyries come from behind me and scatter across the city.

"Farewell, children of man." The Valkyries all shone in unison. I took my opportunity to get the heck out of dodge through a portal, and hid away from sight. After the light faded, I created another illusion of beautiful feathers falling from the sky. I felt like I was directing a movie.

The pope then rose to her feet.

"God has left! From now on, we will take full responsibility for our actions! We will repent as one, for betraying God's will! As He spoke, we should all have taken in a message of accountability! We will work hard and seize what is right with our own hands! Pray to Him in gratitude and peace!"

The voices of the people roared across the night, they were elated. That's about what I expected, but... She definitely had more charisma than me, that much was for certain.

I figured that would be enough to let everything work out. As I watched the excited townsfolk and the pope's speech, my smartphone began to vibrate. I seemed to have an incoming call.

"Hello! Is this God?"

"That it is, my boy. Ahaha... it seems you have put the situation to rest! I am quite relieved, thank you."

"Yup, seems like we'll be fine now. Any weird stuff that was interfering with their minds should die down soon enough, if not already. Now the people should be able to make rational decisions for themselves." In a sense, you could say that I had driven a divide in the people's minds about the concept of God itself. The influence of Ramissh was likely to decrease after this, but… In turn, the people oppressed by their wicked justice would go down as well.

There would surely still be those who believed in Lars, god of light, but that was fine by me. Believing or not was ultimately their choice, and that just meant they were human. All I had done was prevent people from abusing that belief and imposing it upon others through force or trickery.

"I do apologize for leaving the matter to you… Do apologize to the young priestess and that charming young popess for me, would you?"

"Don't worry about it. Just pay me back by looking in on their country now and then, just in case things get weird again."

"Very well, then! I'll be sure to pay attention." I hung up on God, and moved back to Phyllis and Kohaku through one of my portals.

"Thank you, Your Highness… Thank you so much." Phyllis was moved to tears the moment she saw me, and respectfully bowed her head. I didn't really do much to deserve that level of appreciation though, if you'd have asked me, I'd say I was the one responsible for the mess to begin with!

"God told me to apologize to you and the pope on his behalf. I think there'll be tough times ahead, do you think you'll be okay?"

"I do. After all, God is always watching." Phyllis nodded, there was no hesitation in her eyes. It seemed I had nothing to worry about.

Since it was through my own magic that various buildings and the grand temple were annihilated, I quickly decided to rebuild them with another of my trusty spells. However, the pope appeared and stopped me in my tracks. She said that showing my power like that in public, especially after everything that had just happened, would be a terrible idea. She had a point, I didn't want to expose the truth behind that God.

I watched over the pope beginning her new type of sermon, and I smiled. I had decided that my work here was done. Though, just in case, I gave Phyllis a Gate Mirror for quick and easy communication. Then, after a short goodbye, Kohaku and I portalled our way home to Brunhild.

Some days later, rumors finally began flowing through various countries that a God had descended in the Ramissh Theocracy, slaying a wicked Dark God in the process. Irreligious countries laughed off the story as propaganda. That aside, the Ramissh Theocracy officially changed their following from Lars, god of light, to simply preaching the word of "god's light." Their motto of it all being in the name of light and justice was also stricken from the record.

Officially, the founder of Ramissh was still Ramirez, and the one that aided him was the god of light. That part of the story remained consistent. All I and the pope had done together was remove any mention of Lars, and his twisted justice.

"Geez, I never expected you to pretend to be a God, Touya... you're gonna get punished from above!" Elze nudged me in the side, laughing at my tale. I had, naturally, explained to my family what had happened in the Theocracy. I just cut out the parts about the real God.

Cardinal Zeon, Cardinal Kyurei, the Templars, and the others who had actively abused the pope were stripped of land, position, and property. They were excommunicated from the church and jailed.

The confiscated wealth ended up being vast, it seemed that all their fearmongering and donation-begging had paid off well for them. The pope kindly returned that money to the people, compensating the victims of years of oppression.

All of those imprisoned also happened to be those that knew the truth behind the Ramissh religion, but it was unlikely they'd be believed even if they did blab. After all, they were all personally judged by God himself before a great crowd.

And, after a short time, an envoy from Ramissh came to greet me in my castle. My halls were graced by the presence of the youngest cardinal in history, Phyllis.

"You seem well."

"As do you, Grand Duke." I took a look at the letter she had brought with her. To be blunt, the letter stated that they were sorry about the previous envoy, and wished to establish good terms with Brunhild.

There was no outlandish demand like forcing me to adopt a state religion, or baptize myself. It was simply a letter of good faith, asking that my duchy maintain a friendship with the Theocracy going forward.

Naturally, I accepted. In order for my country to grow, good diplomacy was necessary and welcome. I had no desire to connect with bad nations, but I had made good friends within the Theocracy.

"Hm, I was somewhat worried just now, but it seems to have ended well... I wonder if the God who appeared in Ramissh intended for this to happen..." After Phyllis left, old man Kousaka let out a small sigh of relief and gave me that comment, along with a sidelong glance.

I didn't tell him the exact details of what went down that day, but I did tell him I was there when it happened. As far as he knew

I was visiting the Theocracy, then God happened to descend. It was mighty convenient, but that was the story I stuck to.

"Do you believe in God, Kousaka?"

"Who can say… He exists within the hearts of those who believe, and does not within the hearts of those who do not. That is what I believe, at least." James Barrie, an English writer, wrote in "Peter Pan" that whenever a child says "I don't believe in fairies," a single fairy dies somewhere.

Kousaka had a point. To believe in something, was to give it life. I don't think anyone could get in the way of that.

"And what of you, Grand Duke? Do you believe in God?"

"I do. I do." Somewhere, off on the breeze outside, I thought I heard the gentle chuckling of the divine old man himself.

"I wanna soar through the sky!"

"That's a little, uh…" Leen and I sat on the balcony. As she sipped her black tea, she raised an eyebrow at my statement.

I'd been thinking about what happened in Ramissh a few days prior, and also what had happened during the coup before that. Both of those events had involved airborne enemies, and it'd make a world of difference if I was freely able to fly around on their level.

Sure, I could just summon a Griffin and ride it around, but flying myself was way cooler than just fighting atop the back of a mythical beast. That's why I decided to ask Leen if she knew anything about it.

"I mean… you can make yourself leap through the sky using wind magic, but… You wouldn't be able to soar or fly freely, nothing like that. It's more of a spell for blasting people away, so you'd just be using the knockback. Less flying, more being blasted away."

"Hrmph… in that case, isn't there a Null spell or something?"

"It's possible. But it's not a Null spell that I know." *Hrmph… I guess fairies wouldn't need flight magic, so none of them bothered memorizing which spell that might be.*

I quickly considered another angle as well. Null magic was personal magic. It's not like most people would be able to use it, even if it was shared. That's probably why looking into it would end up being fruitless.

Guess I've got no choice, then. I'm gonna have to look through those dusty old magic books. I'd bought a ton of encyclopedias about Null magic from various bookstores, and gotten them together in the castle's library. The books had records of Null magic from all over the world, and from various periods in time. But, since it was a comprehensive list, the spells ranged from useful... to absurdly useless. One of the spells allowed you to make ants walk in a straight line. I couldn't even think how anyone discovered that, or why. "Touya, bruv... you're really gonna look through all of this?" Renne was free, so I asked her to help out. But after looking at just one book, she seemed intimidated. I guess she had a point...

The worst thing about all of these books is that they were all published independently of each other, and at different points in time. Therefore I saw a lot of repeated spell names in each book. [Gate] was apparently pretty well-known. It was listed in every one.

"Yep, I think so. Gonna scour them all. Let's have Lain and Cesca help us out later on." Renne sat on a chair and began to look through the books. While we were ostensibly searching for magic that'd allow me to fly, I also asked her to keep an eye out for any spell that might seem useful as well.

I thought maybe the spell would be called [Fly], or [Flight], but even if I invoked those names, nothing happened. I wasn't entirely sure why that was the case, but it was probable that I needed to fully understand the effects of the spell before I could visualize and use it.

I wondered now and then, but my power felt more like a copy ability than anything else. I replicated magic that already existed, and made it my own. I never really created my own.

I decided thinking about stuff like that was a bit pointless, though. As I flipped through the books, I found some interesting spells now and then. Like [Taboo] a spell that censored certain words and made it impossible to speak them. That was interesting, but I didn't know exactly how useful it'd be. For example, I could forbid the use of the word [Fireball], and that might prevent my enemy from casting that spell, but it looked like the effect was limited to one word per person.

"Oi bruv, what about this one?"

"...Nope, don't need that one." What Renne had found was a spell named [Mosaic]. I wasn't sure about it... Apparently it was a kind of spell that interfered with the visual spectrum and allowed you to blur certain objects in people's field of view, but... all it made me think of was something sexually obscene. It confused me, because mosaics were supposed to be a pattern-based art form! I had no idea why it created that kind of effect.

Other spells included [Silence], a spell that made things quiet. [Speaker], which made everything noisy... and [Shield], which created an invisible barrier to defend the user.

Luckily it hadn't been a complete waste of time, I'd found a few useful spells. [Silence] didn't actually prevent spells from being cast, like I'd thought it might. It just made the chanting inaudible, they could still be cast even under the effects of the spell.

Regardless, we still hadn't found what we were looking for to begin with...

"Oho." My hand stopped on a certain page.

[Levitation]. It was a spell that allowed objects to float. But it seemed to only make things float within arm's reach of the caster. I figured it'd be around two meters, then. Meaning it'd be a useful spell for carrying stuff, but I already had [Storage] for that anyway. Then again, I couldn't use [Storage] on living creatures, so it could end up being useful after all.

"[Levitation]." As a test, I decided to use the spell on the book. The heavy old tome started floating up in the air. *Whoa, it really is floating!* I tried moving it around in the air. *Yup, it can move, but...* As I'd expected, it couldn't move any further than my own reach.

I applied [Levitation] to Renne as another test, but it looked like she couldn't move freely in the air. She motioned like she was swimming, but only budged a tiny bit. I wondered if propelling her with a fan or something would work... Renne seemed like she was having fun, but it wasn't really something you could call flying. She couldn't go beyond two meters, and she was crawling at a snail's pace. But seeing her did make me wonder if I could enchant it into a rug and make a flying carpet like in Arabian Nights. "I guess I'll memorize this one for the time being." The magic seemed like it had potential, I just had to learn how to apply it properly.

When the afternoon rolled around, Cesca and Lain came to help us. With the power of four, our speed was increased considerably. After just two hours, Cesca finally found it.

"[Fly]. The method to propel oneself with magic. Indeed, this must be it. It seems that the spell consumes a considerable amount of magical power, but I doubt that'll be an issue." According to the book, the person who originally used this spell could freely fly for a maximum of three minutes. But apparently when it was over, he came crashing toward the ground. I doubted that'd be an issue for me, I had the convenient power of teleportation portals, after all. Three seconds were enough to regain enough magic to create one.

Either way, I'd have to test it out. That was the first step.

I arrived at the training field and began to concentrate my magical energy. Renne, Cesca, Lain, Nikola, and Elze were all watching me. The latter two took a break from their training to come over and watch. Old man Yamagata and company also came over. It was a little distracting. But regardless of the attention, I had to focus.

"[Fly]." My body suddenly began to float about one meter above the ground. It was awesome. My body turned without me actively willing it, so I figured it was operating on my most basic thoughts, like moving a limb. I decided to try going up a little higher, but the moment that thought entered my mind, I shot several meters up in the air! *Uwaaah!* The fine-tuning left much to be desired. It kind of felt like I was operating one of those RC Helicopters, but without a controller. After a while, I was up way too high for comfort, though. I'd tried seeing how high I could go, but had to stop when the air became so thin and cold that I started losing feeling in my limbs. I thought I was gonna suffocate!

The next test was working out my maximum speed. But again, I had to stop. The wind on my face was extreme, way too extreme! I had to close my eyes and fly blind for a while.

Hrmph... maybe this'll be tricky to deal with. Should I use [Shield], *maybe?* I put up a barrier, and it worked as a makeshift windscreen. *Yup, that works.*

After that, I decided to try turning around. I started zig-zagging, stopping suddenly, nosediving, somersaulting! It was actually really fun. *Alright, let's try three spinning somersaults!*

I got a little carried away...

"...You tried spinning around in the air and you're surprised you got queasy?!"

"I-I don't really have an excuse." I was completely exhausted, lying down beneath a tree with my head on Elze's lap. I'd calmed down some, but the incident itself was still a little extreme for me.

I didn't even know why I'd done it, I hated riding stuff like rollercoasters. High-speed stuff like that definitely wasn't my scene.

Come to think of it, the Great Gau River ride left me feeling kinda seasick, too...

For whatever reason, [Recovery] didn't alleviate queasiness like this. When Baba got drunk on sake, I tried using that spell on him as a sort of field test. It sobered him up right away, which I found hilarious. *Then again, I guess being drunk on sake and dizzy on motion sickness are two different things.* Incidentally, old man Baba started drinking booze right after he sobered up.

"Were there any other problems?"

"Nah, it was pretty much fine. I did get super cold when I went way up high, though..." *Come to think of it, I could probably use* [Warming] *to negate the cold. But the atmosphere's way too thin up there, and it's not like I was looking to explore space anyway.*

I raised my head and sat up properly, I didn't intend to use her as a lap pillow forever. *Hm, stuff like this has gotten less embarrassing lately. We probably look like one of those annoying lovey-dovey couples at this point, huh...*

"Hey, Touya... Do you think you could use that magic on me? Would I be able to fly then?"

"No, I don't think it's possible. I can't use my magic in that way. You can't put [Boost] on Linze, right? It's the same thing."

"I guess so..." Elze let out a sad sigh. I think she wanted to fly with me.

"You should be able to fly if I hold you in my arms, though."

"A-Ah, that's… p-pretty embarrassing." Elze turned beet red and looked down nervously. *So lap pillows are fine, but being held isn't? I don't get the criteria here!*

"You might be able to fly by my side if I used [**Levitation**] as well, but you wouldn't be able to fly freely in that case." I tried to make Elze float using one of my newfound spells. She was caught by surprise and tried to flail around, which was a little funny. After she calmed down, I tried levitating her around. As expected, she stopped around about where my arms could reach.

"[**Fly**]." I used my flying spell after that. As I rose, Elze rose with me. I'd figured it out. I'd be able to raise people up and down based on my own location in the air. So long as I paid attention, I could use [**Levitation**] to make people fly alongside me.

I took care to maintain everything, and flew up to the castle balcony. *Yup, no problem!* Elze staggered around and put her hand to her chest, letting out a sigh of relief.

"That was scary! I-I'm still not used to it. M-Maybe I don't need to fly after all…" Heh, that was amusing. But I could understand. Her movements were beyond her control, and if she fell from that height she'd definitely die.

That aside, my mission was complete. This new spell changed the game for me. Creatures like the Manta Phrase no longer had air superiority over me.

"I'm gonna go fly again."

"Okay, don't get sick this time." Elze waved me off, and I circled the castle a few times. After that, I flew across the highway. Looking down on the town from above, it was easy to see it'd been expanded considerably. It was quite an emotional sight, if I'm honest.

Still, it did look more like a shopping district than a full town… I touched down in a back alley, where I'd noticed a few children playing with spinning tops.

"Uwaaah?! M-Milord?! Wh-What a surprise!"

"Did you just come out of the sky?!"

"Th-That's amazing!" It was a little heart-warming to see the kids look up to me. I didn't want them to revere me too hard, though.

"What?! Do you dare think a goddamn sorry is enough? After treating a customer like this?!" A crude male voice echoed from across the street. I looked over from where it came from, and there seemed to be a commotion going on in a coffee shop.

Two large men stood on the shop patio. They looked like military-types. More importantly, they were hassling a waitress.

"Lookie here! There's a goddamn cigarette butt in my food! How can you expect me ta pay for that?!"

"You better compensate us, bitch! What if we ate it?! What if we got a tummy ache?! Good thing we're so goddamn attentive, understand?!" Those guys were assholes. They totally looked like crooks. I had no doubt they were lying.

I walked over to the shop and spoke to the waitress.

"Something wrong here?"

"A-Ah, these two gents say there's a cigarette butt in their food, but… Nobody who works here actually smokes, so I don't understand!"

"Hear that, boys? Sounds like you're mistaken. Sure neither of you dropped it in the food by mistake?" The waitress stood behind me, and I puffed out my chest. The two men glared daggers at me.

"Huh? What's it ta you, fuckface? You looking down on us, brat? Who the hell're you?"

"Yeah, you little shitbird. Want a first-class ticket to paintown? Step right up, bitch." The two men loomed in closer as they cracked their knuckles. *Well. Let's have a little fun, then.*

I touched the men on their arms, pushed them, and they fell back easily. They flew away from the shop and landed in the middle of the road.

"Ghuh!!"

"Aghagh!!" They flew pretty easily, but that was because I'd reduced their weight with [Gravity]. Neither of them seemed to understand what had just happened, but they charged at me regardless. One brandished an axe, the other held a broadsword.

"[Slip]."

"Augh!"

"Eek!" The two men went tumbling down. Then, I used [Gravity] to keep them down. They were completely immobilized by their own increased body weight, so I strolled over, grinned, and squatted down near them.

"A-Augh… h-how…!"

"I'd really appreciate it if you didn't cause trouble in my country. I can't really overlook things like this, given that I kind of run the show around here. Understand?"

The two men looked at each other in shock, their expressions shifting in fear. The surprise coating their faces acted as proof that they understood who I was. *Bah, these guys are a real pain in the ass. What should I do with them?*

Actually, we don't have a prison or anything yet, do we… Guess I should take this opportunity to set one up.

I took out several iron pieces from [Storage] and created a decently-sized prison room. After that, I applied a few enchantments, and a [**Program**]. Then, after stripping them of their gear, I tossed the two men inside.

I called it a prison, but it was just an iron box with one see-through wall. There were no bars, either. I wasn't a monster, though. I'd put airholes in the ceiling!

Now, let's begin the punishment! The moment the door closed, the two of them began to scream and yell. At least, it looked like that's what they were doing. I'd soundproofed the cell. The two of them were running around the interior of the prison, clutching at their ears and roaring in what looked like extreme discomfort. Despite the commotion going on in there, not a single sound leaked out. I'd enchanted the cell with [**Silence**] after all.

"M-Milord... what's going on in there?"

"Mm, just a little crash course in white noise."

"Err, noise?"

"There's a sound blaring in there at a similar frequency to nails coming down a chalkboard, and a fork scratching against a plate. Over, and over, and over again."

"O-Oh goodness me..." The waitress slinked back a little, a dash of fear clouding her eyes as she looked at me, and then the floor. *What's her problem?*

Eventually the guardsmen came running over. I set it so the sound would stop when the door was opened, so I handed the key over to them, placed the jail in a good position, and told them to let the guys out whenever they felt it appropriate.

Seeing that commotion made me realize that there was a lot more to work on in my country. *I definitely need to improve defenses and public order infrastructure... Maybe I should finally get around to establishing my knight order.*

I flew off toward the castle, pondering my next course of action.

"…And that's why I think we need to establish our knight order." Everyone sat around the conference table, but only Kousaka stood up after I made my case.

"Given our current national interests, I believe I have a reasonable plan set out, then. For our knights, we shall start with thirty ex-Takeda troops. They were originally our subordinates, so we've already vetted them extensively. Fifteen of Baba's men, fifteen of Yamagata's. On top of that, we will integrate ten former Takeda ninjas, commanded by Tsubaki, to create our intelligence corps. In addition, we should take sixty new recruits, giving us a nice round one hundred. What are your thoughts?" Sixty new recruits sounded good to me. The town wasn't especially large, so it sounded like a good start.

Aside from myself, the conference room was occupied by Baba, Yamagata, Naito, and our chief ninja Tsubaki. Lain, Nikola, and Norn were also present. Kousaka, Naito, and Tsubaki weren't really knights, but it made sense to include them on military matters.

"So what are the qualifying traits we want in a recruit?" Old man Baba spoke up with a question, to which I replied immediately.

"Well, let's see… I'll reject anyone with a criminal background right off the bat. Sex doesn't matter. Race doesn't matter. Neither social standing nor age matter, either."

"Isn't that a tad broad? Won't we get a swarm of candidates in that case?" Yamagata had a point, but I decided that taking a ton of applications gave us a better chance of finding talented people.

The mission here was to separate the wheat from the chaff, and find the diamonds in the rough.

"Who's going to be the commander, anyway?" Naito raised his hand and let out an innocent enough question. *Oh, I never thought about that.* I cast a cursory glance over at Yamagata and Baba. "I'm sorry, my boy, but… I won't be taking that role. Squad captain's more than enough for me."

"Same here. It ain't in my nature to take such a demanding job." *Welp, it was worth a shot.* I had hoped that one of them would accept, since they had served as generals for Takeda and all, but… I guess they'd had enough of that life. *Well, that just leaves…*

"I'll have to pick one of you three, then."

"Wait, us?!" Lain's rabbit ears perked up rapidly. Norn and Nikola just stared, dumbfounded. I didn't know what they were so surprised about. The wolf, rabbit, and fox trio were formal knights of my kingdom, after all.

"Well, there's nobody else."

"B-But we can't be commanders, that's impossible!" Lain waved her hands in a fluster all of a sudden. The two behind her nodded in unified agreement.

"Well, I mean, in the case of emergencies you three band up with me anyway, right? I just think it's necessary to have a commander while I'm absent. Plus, it's only a company of one hundred."

"That's true, but…" Having a commander was necessary. Even if it didn't have that many members, I needed to maintain a hierarchy. But the issue was which of them to choose. They were all talented, but all had their drawbacks too.

Nikola was stoic and serious, but generally inflexible. Norn was a people person, but very reckless. Lain was an exemplary all-rounder, but she was dangerously reserved.

"Look, for now let's have one of you be the commander, and the other two can be the vice-commanders. Alright?" Nikola immediately raised his hand.

"Lain should be the commander, then."

"Y-Yeah, I agree! Lain'll do great!"

"Wh-Wh-What?!" Lain was betrayed by her closest comrades! She glared right at them. But she was outvoted two-to-one, so I was completely fine to go ahead with it.

"U-Um, please, you two...! Isn't Nikola more suited for the role than I?!"

"Nah, you're much better for this. Norn's careless, so she'd make a sloppy commander. She likes to slack off, too. I'm kind of a strict person, so I don't think I'd treat people especially fairly. Inflexibility is not a trait you want at the head of an organization. They say a carrot and a stick is needed to drive something forward, but I'm just a stick. I'd say that you're the carrot we need, Lain." *Hm, lemme look at this objectively here...* This case kind of reminded me of the Hijikata Toshizo, vice-commander of the Shinsengumi. He was known as the Demon Vice-Commander because of his attitude. So while Kondo Isami took the role as the Shinsengumi's commander, Toshizo simply stood by the wayside and sternly enforced the rules. A guy like that was definitely best at the side-lines, growling and staring.

"Very well, then. Lain's the new commander."

"Sounds good to us!"

"Wh-What?! Please wait a moment!" All three of them had grown considerably stronger over the last few months. Yamagata and Baba had really put them through the wringer, and the results were showing. They'd even trained often with veterans from both Regulus and Belfast. They all had valiant personalities, and they were naturally talented in the physical arts just by virtue of being beastmen.

That aside, putting Lain at the top of my knight order was a convenient social move, as well. She was a beastwoman, so that was two birds with one stone. With Lain as the commander, everyone would know at a glance that Brunhild was a progressive country that did not discriminate based on sex or race.

"Please don't worry so much. Even if the title is commander, right now it's only comparable to leading a small platoon. Don't get worked up, you'll be fine. Your two vice-commanders will be supporting you fully as well."

"Yessir."

"You got it!" Nikola stood stoic and serious, while Norn gave a bubbly response. Lain just sat down on her chair, staring blankly and quietly babbling. Her rabbit ears were drooped down in resignation.

It felt a little awkward, but I'm sure she'd do her best. I also decided to support her in every way possible.

All that was left was to create leaflets and fliers, then distribute them. I was sure that putting them in places like the guild in Regulus and Belfast would be more than enough.

We all decided to host the interview itself after a month.

And then, one month later...

"Huh?"

"Allow me to repeat myself. Over a thousand candidates are here to fill up the sixty available positions. It is both unexpected and unprecedented." Kousaka repeated himself, but I still couldn't wrap my head around what he said. How had we attracted that many people? Sure, we'd thrown out fliers all over the place, but over a thousand, really? There were more applicants than citizens!

"How did this happen?"

"Your Highness... you are the sole Silver-ranked adventurer in Belfast. You squashed a military coup in Regulus. You slayed a Dragon in Mismede! These people were naturally drawn here due to your great deeds. Word of mouth is powerful. But of course there are likely spies from other nations mixed in amongst the candidates as well." That made sense enough. It was still better to have a ton of candidates than no candidates, though. "How do you plan on processing them, then? And what about the criteria you're looking for in a knight?"

"Hrmm, I'm not actually sure about the best course of action. I still haven't got that figured out." I didn't know the first thing about interviewing this many people.

"Well, Your Highness... it depends on the kind of individual you want to prioritize within the ranks of Brunhild. Frankly, if you think strength is all that matters, why not have them all brawl until there are only sixty left? Hohoh..." *Easy for you to say. Well, if they're thuggish or crude I don't want them working here. I guess the ideal I'm looking for in a knight is someone who looks at the citizens and sees them as the priority. Good-hearted people with dutiful attitudes. I'm sure a lot of people will have come along with different expectations, but I'm not gonna budge there.*

Still, interviewing each candidate one after the other is gonna be a pain. What should I do...

"Applicants for the Brunhild knight order, please come over here. Line up in an orderly fashion." The desk was at the castle gates. I had the applicants come one by one to write down their full name, their sex, their age, birthplace, race, and personal statements on a document. After that, Lapis would give them a numbered badge. Then, that same number was stamped on the back of their hand. The actual interview was scheduled for two days afterward.

The badges were to be worn on the chest, or anywhere where it was easily visible. Wearing them was mandatory.

The badges were secretly the first part of the test. I'd informed every citizen of the town to record the badge number of anyone that gives them a tough time or a poor impression. I asked them to put down the reason for the concern, and the nature of the harassment.

A smart applicant would probably realize the meaning behind the badge to begin with.

This wasn't a test to find those with the right qualities, but more of a test to root out those with the wrong qualities. Those who were inconsiderate, those who didn't think about the badge's meaning, or the people they were going to be protecting? I didn't want those people anywhere near my country.

I used [**Mirage**] on Tsubaki's subordinates to make them look like demonkin and beastmen, then I had them wander around the town. I wanted to see if anyone would actively discriminate against them. Because those were the kind of people I wanted to kick out.

About a third of the candidates were demi-human, so naturally if I employed them I wanted them working alongside people who wouldn't discriminate or look down on them. It'd be a pain in the ass if I had people who were like, "Wow, you're okay for a beastman," as well. Friendly discrimination was still racist.

I summoned one hundred cats and sent them into town. Their mission was to report in to me about the situation.

"Meow... there's a certain fellow hassling a merchant! He's badge number six hundred and eighty-five."

"Meow, there's a group of drunkards making a hassle in a restaurant. The barkeep's trying to keep the situation under control, meow! They're badges number eighty-two through eighty-five!"

"S-Some rude son of a meow threw a rock at me... He's badge number two hundred and fifty-eight!" I was surprised that so many reports were coming in so soon. It was pretty hard for me to take note of all of that alone. I decided to ask Kohaku for help. Kohaku was the Monarch that governed land beasts, so that tiger would have no issue receiving telepathic messages from the cats either. Renne and Laim came to help me record everything.

Over a thousand applicants had shown up, so Micah's inn was beyond its limit. In the end, most of the applicants had to camp in the plains outside town. Thankfully there was no dangerous wildlife in the region.

A huge variety of people had shown up, though. I disguised myself with [Mirage] and went to check out the town. There were a lot of female adventurers, probably because I'd mentioned that sex didn't matter. A lot of beastmen and demonkin showed up as well, mostly gathering in groups of their own.

I decided to reject humans that were racist against beastmen and demonkin, but I also decided to reject beastmen and intelligent monsters that were racist toward humans as well. It was true that they might've all had personal circumstances that made them feel that way, but my country had no room for discriminatory people, bleeding hearts or not.

With that initial wave over, the worst of them would probably be singled out and removed. But the screening still had to occur.

My idea of using [Paralysis] on all of the candidates and letting those with high magical resistance pass to the next round was vetoed.

I guess it didn't have much to do with knighthood. It didn't really let me know if the person was good or bad, either.

I decided to rely on Yumina's Mystic Eyes for that little detail, but resolved only to include her after I'd narrowed down the candidates considerably.

Things were definitely about to get busier.

It was screening day. The people whose ticket numbers had been recorded by Tsubaki's subordinates and the cats were not allowed passage through the castle's gate. Of course, some people were hanging around, but most had gone home in low spirits, grumbling to themselves about what they could do to help their country. Thus about fifty people had been rejected, which left about nine hundred and fifty people. But only about a twentieth had left. That wasn't enough.

Applicants gathered within the training ground in the castle. I stood on the hastily constructed stage alongside Lain, Norn, Nikola, Baba, and Yamagata. Elze, Linze, Yae, Yumina, Lu, and Tsubaki all waited in the wings beside the stage.

I used my Null spell **[Speaker]**, which caused the sides of the stages to shine as magic formations headed toward the galleries.

These two magic formations, about thirty centimeters in diameter, floated up into the sky as another smaller formation appeared by my mouth. Anything I'd say into this one would stream out of the larger formations at a magnified volume.

"First, allow me to welcome you all to the Duchy of Brunhild. I am Mochizuki Touya, the grand duke. We are about to proceed with the screening to see who will join my royal knight order. But let me be frank with you all, we do not pay much. As knights you will not only defend this duchy, but you will have numerous other roles to fill as well. As you can see from the beastmen behind me, your race or social position will do you no favors here. I would ask only those who agree with what I've said to remain here." I declared as such, and the applicants began to mutter amongst themselves. Eventually several of them left through the castle gate. Well, I didn't expect everyone to stay after that. If they didn't agree with what I'd said, then I'd much rather have had them leave immediately.

"In that case, I will now have you all show me your strength. Please head out through the gate, and do a lap around the castle moat." A puzzled expression came over the crowd's faces at my latest declaration. The distance around the castle was about two kilometers. They were likely thinking it was too small a distance to test strength.

"It also matters not if you come first or last. I wish you to take this at your own pace. Those who find this too hard and wish to give up are to remove the badges they're wearing. You'll be teleported back here and allowed to leave. With that said, let's begin!" As the applicants began to file off, I cast my magic.

"[Gravity]."

"Argh?!" Everyone collapsed to the ground under their newfound weight.

"I used weight magic on you all. Please complete the course under these conditions. If you wish to give up, simply do as I said earlier and remove your badge. You will then be teleported here." The applicants began to stand up one by one, and then walked slowly out of the gate. They weren't quite going at a snail's pace, but it was far slower than standard walking speed.

I hadn't made them so heavy that they couldn't move, so they should still be able to walk fine. It'd take an incredibly amount of strength though. I'd also sent the ninjas to keep an eye on everyone, in case anyone tried to get sneaky, or accidentally fell into the moat.

"So their position doesn't matter?"

"Hmm... Well I'll take it into consideration, but this isn't a test to simply see their physical strength." I answered Laim's question. I'll certainly be able to work out how strong they are from this. But that isn't what I want to know.

"If this isn't a test of physical strength, then what is it?"

"A test of will."

"Their will?" How serious they can be, in other words. Anyone who gives up immediately wouldn't be any use to us. Those would be the first people to give up when the going gets tough. And that could put us all in danger.

After a certain amount of time had passed, I intended to send relief to those who haven't returned. But anyone who gives up before that would be instantly disqualified. Anyone still striving for the goal at that point would be considered a successful applicant, and move on to the next stage.

I explained all this to Laim as people started teleporting in, having given up. *That's way too soon! At least put some effort into it!*

I removed [Gravity] from them, and used [Refresh] to restore their strength before quickly sending them home. *Hm, how many are left...*

Wow, we started with nine hundred and fifty, but we're already down to four hundred and fifty?! That means half of them have given up already!

The people in first place were all beastmen and demonkin who had naturally enhanced strength, but that wasn't too important here. As long as a person had the mental strength to continue without giving up, they'd pass. Whatever their reason for giving up, be it that they were merely window-shopping for a job, or just realized their own lack of strength, that was irrelevant to me as well. I appreciated their efforts, regardless.

After a certain amount of time elapsed, I used recovery magic on everyone who was still struggling. I also cast it on anyone that managed to make it through the goal.

Now, for the next test.

"Next we'll move onto the practical skills examination. You may use whatever weapons you prefer. Any who manages to land a hit on me within thirty minutes will have passed. I shall be using this wooden sword. You may begin." I declared the start and picked up my wooden sword, but not a single person charged toward me. I was thinking about how weird it was that they weren't doing anything, when eventually someone timidly spoke up.

"U-Uh, what order are we meant to attack you in?" Ahh, so that's it.

"That doesn't matter. You can all come at me at once. Give it everything you've got, by all means." They might've thought I was mocking them, because they all begin to charge me at once, specialized weapons in hand.

"[Accel]." I used my acceleration magic to slip between them, and start hitting the unprotected applicants with my sword. Given the huge number of people, they kept on surging toward me. But I just kept on dodging, hitting out when I got the chance.

I made a point not to attack anyone who held a firm guard. During this test, Baba, Yamagata, Elze and Yae were judging the participants' skills. If they were determined to be above a certain level, then their number would be recorded. I felt bad for the people who I could clearly see weren't at that level, but I hit them anyway. That meant they'd failed.

Occasionally an attack would come my way, but [**Accel**] made it a trifling matter to deal with. Eventually, half of the people had fallen, with the rest still standing raggedly around the field.

"That's enough. Time!" Laim announced the test's end. And with that, everyone collapsed to the ground. That also reminded me, I happened to see a few people I recognized during the brawl.

I glanced over to the two of them, collapsed on the ground. *Ha! Wow, it's Rebecca and Logan.*

They were the two adventurers I'd met in the Rabbi Desert. Last I heard they were still guarding the reading cafe back in Belfast. I wondered what had brought them here. The two of them noticed my staring and gave me a small wave. I wanted to talk to them, but there were a lot of people around. I wouldn't want them knowing that I knew any of the applicants. They might start thinking I was giving people special treatment.

I cast recovery magic on everyone, and took the notes from Baba and the others.

"I'll now read out the results. Those whose numbers I read out will come this way. If I do not read out your number, I apologize, but you have failed. Please leave through the castle gates. I will now begin. Numbers three, fourteen, twenty-one…" Now only one hundred people remained. The people I attacked obviously failed, but so did the ones who didn't try to attack me. This was their chance to show off their own abilities, so that only makes sense.

In addition, both Rebecca and Logan ended up passing. And, since I wasn't the one who decided that, it wasn't like I gave them special treatment or anything.

We sure have narrowed it down… Now there should be few enough for the interview phase.

CHAPTER IV: IMPROVING THE DUCHY

We took the successful applicants into the castle, and headed toward the knights' barracks. Leaving the applicants in one room, we began preparing the adjacent one for the interviews. The ones leading these interviews were to be myself, Laim, Yumina, and one more person. I'd called them to the duchy, because their aid was imperative.

"Sorry for making you come here. Your help is much appreciated."

"Oh no, this is nothing. I already owe you far more than I could ever repay." Her Eminence the Pope smiled as she answered me. I'd contacted the Ramissh Theocracy beforehand to ask for help. Her guards, several holy paladins, were waiting at the back of the room too. We were going to perform these interviews using the pope's ability to see through lies, and Yumina's ability to see one's true nature.

Her Holiness was a bit of a celebrity, so I used [**Mirage**] to disguise her appearance. When I did so, she asked me to make her look young. Since she'd look like a different person I didn't think it really mattered… But a woman's heart could be complicated and fickle, I guess.

"Very well, call them five at a time." Nikola left the room, and came back with five applicants. Two beastmen, and three humans. I advised that they sit in the chairs in the center of the room.

"If you could all state your names, age, and birthplace, from left to right please." Laim and I began to ask rather inoffensive questions as Yumina checked out their true natures.

Every time we asked a question, Her Holiness either clenched or opened her left hand. This was a signal we set up in advance. If she opened her hand flat, it meant they were telling the truth. But if she

179

IN ANOTHER WORLD WITH MY SMARTPHONE

clenched her hand into a fist, then they were lying. I continued to ask questions as I observe this.

It's not that telling a lie will get you immediately disqualified. There are things people don't want to talk about, and things that could be dangerous if revealed. But I cannot place my trust in someone who would lie about everything and anything.

Nor did it mean that people who truthfully answered question such as "What's more important, you or your country?", "What would you do if you were rich?", and "Could you calmly dispose of a traitor?", would immediately pass.

When the interview was done we allowed the five applicants to leave the room before Yumina started to speak.

"We should reject the people third and fifth from the left. I believe they had malicious intent in their minds."

"They did indeed tell many lies. They had wonderful poker faces, however."

"Poker faces…? Ahh, you mean the technique where you stop your opponent from reading your expression during card games." For now we decided to cross those two people off the list, and had Nikola call in the next five. *We're gonna have to do this twenty times? What a pain in the ass…*

"Ahh, I'm exhausted…!" We were finally done with the interviews, which meant my head could come crashing down on the desk. Fighting against a lot of people was far easier, if you asked me.

We ended up dealing with a few people who casually lied with smiles on their faces like it was nothing. It kinda freaked me out. Still, it seemed that the ability to discern lies from truth was actually a bit of a burden.

"I try my best not to invoke it too often. Sometimes it's best not to know." Her Eminence certainly had a point. If you went through life seeing through everyone completely, you could end up mistrusting people in general. I hoped I hadn't made her overdo it a bit. I decided to treat her to dinner later as an apology.

After we rounded off the disqualified candidates, there were sixty-four applicants remaining. It was just a little bit more than expected, but I was fine to accept all of them.

Thirty-seven men, and twenty-seven women. It was actually more women than I had anticipated. Though, it was probably because the knight orders in other countries didn't allow females to join. My poster had specified that sex, creed, or race was irrelevant, so naturally a few talented ladies made their way to my duchy.

As it happened, Rebecca's reason for coming to Brunhild was precisely that. Logan also came along, stating he was looking for steady work. I asked if they were planning on getting married or something, but they both yelled at me in surprised unison. Apparently he was seeing someone else. Talk about awkward…

Twenty-two of the candidates were beastmen and demonkin. I could understand so many beastmen coming in, because my commanding trio were also beastmen, but the number of demonkin definitely threw me off.

Demonkin were a species that were typically bipedal and similar to humans in appearance. But even if they were generally considered demi-human, they were much closer to conventional monsters for the most part. Members of their race included vampires, lamias, ogres, and alraunes. They're fully capable of communication, and are just as intelligent as humans, though they tend to keep their distance from mankind.

As you'd expect, there's a lot of prejudice and discrimination against demonkin across the world. Several countries even actively oppress members of the species, including the Ramissh Theocracy before their reforms.

The interviews with the demonkin were especially strict and thorough due to the potential distrust or ill will toward humanity. But the five of them that passed all were approved wholly by Yumina's Mystic Eyes. Her Holiness the Pope also determined they were all honest and true individuals. They all genuinely wished to live amongst humans, so I passed them. They were a vampire, an ogre, an alraune, and two lamias.

As an aside, the vampire candidate looked like a stereotypical vampire, but he seemed to be fine without drinking blood. Apparently, amongst vampires at least, blood was seen as something similar to how humans see booze or cigarettes. Some enjoyed partaking, but others just had no interest or even actively disliked it. The vampire who joined our ranks stated that he was quite uncomfortable around blood, actually. It was pretty jarring, given my image of vampirism as an insatiable hunger.

I began wondering just how my royal knights were going to end up looking. There were a few details like squad arrangement to go over, but we certainly had quite the diverse cast of characters making up my ranks. I didn't mind, though, it seemed like things would be more fun that way anyhow.

I created a second barrack due to our sudden increase in troops. Men and women didn't need to share accommodation, either. Though I provided the barracks for them to live in, I'd also be fine with them staying in the town if they paid for it themselves.

I also took some advice from old man Baba and built an underground training facility.

"For the time bein', these three're the commander and vice-commanders, right? How's it gonna look to the newbies if they see Yamagata and me beatin' them around?" He had a point. The three of them were definitely strong, but they still weren't tough enough to hold a candle to the old men. If the new recruits saw them getting roughed up by Yamagata and company, they might lose confidence in Lain and consider the old men more suited to lead. That'd be bad!

Therefore we decided to create an elite-members only exclusive training facility, deep underground. As they poured into the place, which was basically just a gym with a training field attached to it, they all looked around in glee at the inventions I had placed within. Like children, they ran over and used the exercise bike, the treadmill, the barbell weights, and so on. They'd end up suffering extreme muscle fatigue if they overdid it. They weren't toys!

Now, I had a few things to do that day. The duchy was being well-managed, so I decided to finally address a few things in my personal life.

Even though it was long overdue, I decided that today was the day... To tell the parents of the girls I'd proposed to that we were engaged.

It was already settled in the case of Yumina and Lu, but I hadn't told Yae's family, or Elze and Linze's, either.

I was already acquainted with Yae's mother and father, but Elze and Linze's biological parents were dead. I knew that their uncle and aunt were living in Refreese though, they lived in a farming village and had raised the twins there.

I decided to meet with Yae's parents first. I whipped up a portal, and the two of us found ourselves in Oedo.

"Been a while since I've been to Eashen." It felt a little funny to me, since roughly half of Brunhild's citizens were Eashen natives. We passed through the gate of the Kokonoe dojo, and Ayane, their maid, came to greet us.

I was brought through to see her parents, Jubei and Nanae. I told them straight-up about my engagement. To my surprise, they didn't respond with much other than a silent glance between the two.

"See? It is as I said it would be."

"I suppose you were correct. Very well, and thank you. Please take care of our Yae as you would your other brides, Touya-dono." They bowed their heads to us, and we returned the gesture. I was kind of pleased it went so seamlessly. I half expected it to turn into a "If you want my daughter, then best me in battle!" kind of a situation.

"But, I must confess... I did not expect you to become nobility, Touya-dono. Nor did I expect my Yae to marry into a monarch's house... life certainly is full of surprises!" Jubei let out his honest feelings. I felt mostly the same as he did. I couldn't have foreseen this happening a year ago.

"Excuse me, Touya-san. Would you perhaps take us to this Brunhild? I wish to see where my daughter will be spending her life."

"Hm? I don't see why not, but bear in mind we aren't very well-developed just yet." I didn't mind if Yae's mother was interested in her daughter's home, so I obliged. We waited for Yae's brother to return home, and I took them all with me. Ayane came along as well, as she'd never seen any place outside of Eashen before.

"Welcome hooome, your Hiiighness."

"Welcome home!" Cecile and Renne came to greet us at the castle entry. Yae's family began to look around at the castle's interior, their heads craning to stare at everything.

"This is Yae's family. They'll be looking around for a while, so please take good care of them."

"Oh myyy, Lady Yae's familyy... This waay, please. I'll shooow you to your quarteeers." Cecile guided them off to their rooms, one-by-one. I decided that we'd stop to have lunch in the dining room, and then take them for a tour around the town. Then again, there wasn't really much to see there. Yae's brother, and her father, would probably prefer to check out our training grounds.

As I expected, they did! I went with the two of them, while Yae went to the castle town with Ayane and Nanae.

The fresh recruits of my knight order were practicing with deadly zeal. I was kind of pleased to see it, because the only thing I'd seen on the training field previously was Lain and the others being beaten to a pulp by old men.

After a short while of observing, Jubei and Jutaro said they wanted to participate in the training as well. That was only natural; they were the direct family of Yae, after all, and she was a sword nut.

I flagged down Yamagata and called him over for a mock battle with Jubei. I thought that a showdown between a former member of the Takeda Elite Four, and the swordsmanship instructor of the Tokugawa house would be something to behold indeed.

As soon as the battle began, everyone was captured by the stunning display of swordplay. Even Jutaro, who was standing right next to me, stood enraptured by the dancing blades.

I watched the two clash for a while, before calling it prematurely. It'd be better for the pride of both men to call it a draw, anyway.

After the battle ended, the knights all clamored around Jubei and begged him to teach them swordplay. I was pleased they were all so eager to improve.

Yamagata then caught the attention of Jutaro, who challenged him immediately. The boy couldn't resist the opportunity to face off against a former member of the Takeda Clan's Elite Four, after all.

He wasn't on his father's level, but Yae's brother certainly put up an incredible fight against old man Yamagata. He was definitely stronger than Lain and the vice-commanders. But he'd been raised with a blade in his hand, and had experienced war as well. If that wasn't natural talent honed through experience, then what was?

The two of them joined the knight recruits and began to practice, which left me with some time to kill. I thought about leaving them in Yamagata's care and heading back to take care of some other stuff, but I had some apprehensions about abandoning what were effectively my brother and father-in-law. I decided it'd be too cold to leave immediately, so I waited around a bit.

As I sat down on the bench and watched them clash, Rebecca walked over to say hello.

"Got some free time, Touya? Oh, er... I mean, my liege, right?" She spoke with a grin plastered on her face. I didn't really mind what she called me, but she should definitely try to act formal with me around other people.

"I didn't expect you to come here at all, Rebecca. Why was it that you came, again?"

"I had aspirations to join an order of Royal Knights. But a woman has little to no chance of joining an order without noble blood, or friends in high places. I started adventuring to hone my skills, then jumped at the chance when I saw the notice about indiscriminate hiring here." That made sense enough to me. There were a lot of women amongst the applicants I'd had. Apparently Logan tagged along after Rebecca invited him. But they had no idea that I was the one at the head of the country.

"Will didn't come, then?"

"He's stuck in Belfast's knight order, I think. Vice-Commander Neil has taken a real liking to him. Plus, Wendy lives over there, so there's no way he'd leave." According to Rebecca, Wendy was still working in Moon Reader, so Will would frequently take guard jobs there.

It was a little late to consider, but I had no idea what was going to happen with that cafe. Would it being owned by the leader of a foreign country be a problem? Well, I had no doubts the King of Belfast would be fine with it either way.

I had them send over reports on revenue, expenditures, and monthly proceeds through a Gate Mirror. I also delivered them new books every month. It was all being managed very well, and seemed to be quite popular. It made me wonder if I'd have to consider setting up a second branch in Brunhild.

"A-Also… I have a request of you, Your Highness…"

"A request?"

"Yeah, see… there should be some equipment that allows one to recognize us as members of the Royal Knights, right? Like a distinctive armor, shield, or blade. Don't you think we should have something like that? Something iconic?" Rebecca blurted out her proposal, blushing slightly. She raised a point I hadn't considered, we definitely didn't have anything unified or distinct. Brunhild's knights would be easier to recognize if they had a piece of gear that made them stand out.

"Hmm… you've got a point, Rebecca! It'd be super convenient if citizens could recognize you as a member of the knight order at a glance."

"For reals, right?!" Rebecca grinned, clapping her hands together. Seems I'd hit it right on the head. She looked way too excited, though. I guess she had always dreamed of joining a royal knight order, though. Plus a stereotypical knight looked very cool and distinct, I figured she wanted to have that kind of image.

"Hmm... then let's give it a try."

"Wait, right now?" I took a lump of mithril out of my magic storage, completely ignoring the bewildered Rebecca as I did so.

I used another of my trusty spells to start shaping it properly. I made an armor plating typical of fantasy anime and games, since I wanted it to have a bit of a different feeling to the armors commonly found in this world.

I made a breastplate, set of shoulder pauldrons, greaves, and neckbrace. I had Rebecca put it on, and then adjusted the size to fit her form. I formed it in such a way that let her have free movement, but also gave the outfit a feminine feeling. Lastly, I made a helmet with a transparent visor and a wide field of view.

I had to make sure it didn't hinder movement, so I had Rebecca go through various motions while wearing it. It was mithril, so it shouldn't have had much weight to it.

"This is amazing! It's like I'm wearing a sheet!" As Rebecca bounded around in the armor a little more, I took a Phrase shard from storage and shaped it into a blade, a shield, and a scabbard. I then charged the items with a small amount of my magic. I also made sure part of the sword's core structure was made of mithril.

The amount of magic I poured into the sword and shield made them harder than mithril itself. I made sure it wasn't as sharp as Yae's Touka, though. Didn't want anyone stealing it and causing absolute chaos with an impossibly sharp blade.

I finished it up by using another nifty spell to reduce the gear's weight. And, just like that, I had created a crystal sword and shield.

It was possible to make armor using the Phrase fragments too, but then it'd be see-through, so I decided against it. I added straps so the shield would be worn on the back, and the sword at the waist, and then it was done.

"So, how is it?"

"Amazing, really!" Rebecca triumphantly held up her shield and thrust out her blade. The glimmering quickly caught the attention of just about everyone else, and soon we were surrounded.

I caught Logan amongst the onlookers, and called him over. Then I used him as a base and took feedback from the other knights to create a male variant of the armor. After that, I went to the workshop and mass-produced the armor for everyone to wear.

Only the base shape was mass-produced, though. I had to apply the enchanted effects myself. Luckily, I had [**Multiple**] to do it all at once.

I set it so the armor intelligently adapted to fit the size of the person wearing it. I also added a crest in the image of Brynhildr, the Germanic shieldmaiden my gun and country were named for, on to the shields.

I made special, unique-looking armors for the commander, vice-commanders, and squad captains. Then I had to create custom-fit armors for the demonkin members of my army. The vampire guy was fine to wear the regular model, though.

It was their on-duty gear, so it would be best if they didn't use it for practice. Their blades were made of Phrase shards, so their magic power would end up depleting if they used it wastefully, and that wouldn't be good…

I returned to the training grounds with the armor in tow. Everyone rushed ahead, desperate to be the first to get their hands on the stuff. They all smiled and began touching at the metal. When they were all fitted in their matching armor, they definitely gave off the feel of a proper group of royal knights.

In later years, due to their swords and shields, Brunhild's knights would come to be known as the "Order of the Crystal Blade." But that's a story for another day.

Ultimately, I was relieved to have the full support of Yae's family, but now I had to go and visit Linze and Elze's family.

"H-Honestly there's no need…" Elze was hesitant for some reason. It seemed that Elze and Linze had sent a letter off that roughly explained the situation. They said they were engaged to the same man, that the man was the ruler of a country, and so on.

Their uncle, who was the younger brother of their mother, owned a farm in a small village called Colette. The village was in the Refreese Imperium, close to Belfast's borders. Elze and Linze lived there until they were twelve years old, when they left in pursuit of independence. Apparently they didn't want to burden their aunt and uncle with too many mouths to feed.

The people of this world sure are independent… In my old world, there are people who leech off their parents well into their twenties… and some that would act as though that was normal.

In any case, if they'd already explained the circumstances, I wanted to at least go and greet the family. I asked them if they'd like to use [Fly] with me and blast off, but they said it was too frightening. *Geez, after all the trouble I went through to learn this spell, too…*

In the end, I just bit the bullet and used [Recall] on Linze to see Colette village, and then we all went there through a [Gate].

I could see what looked to be an orchard off in the distance. There were red fruits dangling from the trees.

The area very much felt like the countryside. There was a big fence erected around the perimeter, though.

I wondered if wild boars came along and ruined crops or something... There was a large house with a red roof in the distance. It was very big, and had a well-aged, rustic feel to it.

"Been a long time since we've been here..."

"It hasn't changed a bit." We wandered over toward the red-roofed house, while the two girls stared at the scenery. There was nostalgia clouding their eyes, so I figured this must be the place.

Two people were tending the field in front of the house. One of them, a man, raised his head and peered over at us. He was wearing a stereotypical farmer's straw hat.

"What...? Elze? Linze?!"

"Yo, long time no see, Uncle Joseph!"

"It's been a while, uncle." Elze and Linze raised their hands to wave at him. The other person who was tending the field, a young woman, raised her head as well.

"Elze, Linze?! Well butter my biscuit, you're home?!" Her face blossomed into a beaming smile. She charged across the field and pulled the twins into a big hug. Her hair was long and brown, all tied up into a braid. She only seemed to be about twenty... *Is this seriously their aunt?!* "Heya sis. We're home!"

"We're home, Emma. It's nice to see you again."

"Geez Louise, you two never came back even once. Even after ya promised to!" Elze must've realized that I was very much left out here, because she parted from the embrace.

"Touya, this is sis. Her name's Emma, though. She's uncle's daughter, and our cousin." *Cousin? Hm, I see... She does kinda look similar to them... I wonder if Elze and Linze'll grow up to look similar to her.*

As I got lost in thought, Elze and Linze's uncle removed his straw hat and strode over. He had beady eyes and white hair, he looked to be around fifty years old as well. He gave off the vibe of a simple country bumpkin, but not in a bad way.

"Ah, I'm happy y'both decided ta come back a bit. Everyone's gonna be real happy. Who's this nice lookin' fella with you, anyhow?" Their uncle looked at me, then Linze, then Elze. He crooked a brow.

"We sent that letter, didn't we? This is Mochizuki Touya. H-He's uhm... ah... h-haha... h-he's our uh... f-f-future hu... huh...!!"

"He's our fiance." The two turned beet red as they gave my introduction to their uncle. *Geez, you two... if you start going on like that you're gonna make me blush as well!*

"...Oh. The letter... right. So this feller's from that Duchy of Brunhild that everyone's been gabbin' on about these days?"

"Indeed. I am the grand duke of the Duchy of Brunhild. My name is Mochizuki Touya. Touya is my given name. I'm indebted to Elze and Linze for their kindn—"

"Wh-Whaaaat?!! Oh my goodness me...!" Their uncle suddenly dropped to the ground and prostrated before me. *What the hell? I only reached out for a handshake.*

"Ahhh, damn it. This is exactly what I thought was gonna happen...!"

"...Typical." Elze and Linze looked at each other with wry smiles. They let out little sighs. Their uncle refused to budge from his prostrated position, he looked like he was quivering, even. I didn't really know what to do, when suddenly Emma started to speak.

"Pops here is pretty uncomfortable and weak-willed when it comes to nobility an' such. Apparently somethin' happened when he was a kid so he gets like this whenever there's someone of a higher status nearby." *What, wait... don't just brush it off! This is beyond "uncomfortable!" He's clearly concealing some kind of traumatic event! Seriously! I'm concerned about what happened to this guy when he was little!*

"Y-Your Most Esteemed Highness, Sir Mochizuki Touya. I am so privileged and emboldened by your presence in my humble home. I am so sorry, I don't have anything to amuse you with, but I respectfully ask that you keep calm... please don't punish us for our transgressions." *This is... weird. Really goddamn weird. Does he think I'm some kind of ticking time bomb?* I turned my head to Linze and Elze, raising a brow at them. They just kind of shrugged and did nothing. *Little help, guys?*

"Oi, dad. You're offending him. Get up already."

"O-Offending him?! I-I'm so sorry, milord! Please forgive me, have mercy!" He rocketed to his feet with a boundless energy and began to talk in a fluster. Now I understood why Elze was so reluctant to bring me here. This guy was something else. I decided not to torment him any further, and moved aside to talk with Emma.

"Sorry... I came here to introduce myself to the family, but is he going to be alright?"

"Don't sweat it. Pop's just like that. Everyone'll be real happy to meet you, honest. Come meet momma an' the others, too." *The others?* I was caught off-guard by what she said, and before I could process the meaning...

"They were telling the truth! Elze and Linze're home!"

"Welcome baaack!"

"Hurray!! The sisters're back! It's Linze an' Elze!" *Whoa...* The rambunctious little tykes came flooding over and embraced the twins. *One… Two… three… six little kids! Two boys and four girls, it looks like.*

I stared on, dumbfounded, while Emma gave a little laugh.

"These are my brothers and sisters. Going from oldest to youngest, there's Sheena, Allen, Kurara and Kirara, Allan, and Reno. They all have an older brother, who's just a bit younger than me, his name's Aaron. But he left for the big city a while back." *Eight kids, for reals? That poor uncle…* It now made sense why Elze and Linze decided to leave so young, they must've felt like they were further burdening an already bustling household. Just thinking of the food expenses this place must've had made my head spin.

Aside from Allen and Allan, they were all girls. Kirara and Kurara looked like they were twins, too. Back in my world they'd say that a family with twins typically had a lot of twins in it. I wondered if the same was said in this one.

I looked over toward the house, and a stout, chubby woman came sauntering out.

"Well I'll be damned… is that Elze and Linze?! Get over here, you rapscallions!"

"Auntie Lana!"

"Yes, it's us. We're home, Aunt Lana." Elze and Linze both ran up to the woman and gave her a big hug. It was their aunt, apparently. She was a chubby, portly woman. But she exuded a lot of character.

Lana patted the two on the head with a warm smile, then she turned to me.

"You must be Touya, then. You're exactly as the two described you in their letter… you certainly seem quite a good man! Ohoho, the two of them certainly described their beloved fiance quite well."

"A-Auntie Lana!"

"...Keep that secret, we mentioned so in the letter." The two of them turned beet red as they voiced their irritation to their aunt. I was curious about what it was they'd written, but opted not to pursue it. I had a feeling it'd just get me in trouble.

"It's a pleasure to meet you, I'm Mochizuki Touya. Touya's my given name."

"My name's Lana. I'm the twins' aunt. You're rather humble for royalty, aren't you?"

"Ahaha... well, I can't really afford not to be. I haven't exactly been noble for long, anyway." Unlike her husband, Lana seemed a bit more confident. She was really friendly and quite the chatterbox. I wondered if this was a case of polar opposites attracting.

"I was nervous when I heard that the two of them would be marrying into royalty, but it seems my fears were unfounded. I can see it in their eyes that you're a good man."

"Thank you for your kindness." Lana's words put me at ease a little. Just then, a little boy who looked to be about seven years old (I think his name was... Allen, or something.), tottered over and tugged at his mother's apron.

"Mommy... is that man royalty?"

"Sort of, sweetheart. He's the grand duke of Brunhild. A country far away from here."

"Wow... is he strong? Can he beat up the Thunderbears?"

"...Thunderbears?" I recalled them as being magical beasts that fired lightning from their bodies. They were a monster usually assigned to Blue Rank guild members, so they were two tiers lower than my Silver Rank.

"Are there Thunderbears around here?"

"Ah, there've been some alleged sightings lately. They say that lightning strikes have been firing out in the dead of night lately, up

195

in the mountains. The crops have been damaged by the occasional fire, so the villagers in the area pooled their money and put out a quest in the guild." I didn't even consider that there'd be problems like farms being collaterally damaged. That sounded like an issue that could become pretty dire if it went unchecked. Not only that, but if the monsters were close enough to damage the fields, then it'd only be a matter of time before people started getting hurt, or worse. I wondered how many monsters there were. I remembered hearing that they were solitary animals and didn't group up much. It was likely there'd just be a couple of them, and maybe some cubs.

However, I'd heard about a special type of Thunderbear that had a strange set of spines running along its back from head to tail. It somehow used this to command other Thunderbears.

If one of those things was involved, it could easily create a large group of Thunderbears. In that case, the quest would immediately jump to a Red Rank, which is a far cry from blue.

"When exactly did you submit the quest to the guild?"

"Three days ago. We don't have a guild here, so we forwarded the request to the nearest large town, Senka. We're fairly sure the quest should be available in the guild by this time tomorrow." Assuming the quest was received and accepted the following day, it'd still be another three or four days until the adventurer who took it actually arrived in the village. I decided to strike while the iron was hot, and prevent further calamity. Contacting the guild afterward would be fine, surely.

"I'll take care of your Thunderbear problem."

"Your Highness, really? Are you sure you'll be alright?"

"I'll be fine. Despite my appearance, I'm a Silver Rank adventurer, after all." I took out a small silver card from my pocket and showed it to Lana, who looked positively dumbfounded. Naturally, I wasn't going to take the reward money from the village, either. I decided to defeat it quickly and get outta there.

"Do you want us to come, too?"

"No. You and Elze have a lot to discuss with your uncle and the others, so I'll tackle this one solo." I declined Linze's offer and floated up into the air with my flight magic. The children looked up at me, gasping in amazement and putting their hands over their mouths. With their wonder backing me, I turned toward the mountains and flew away.

After landing up on the mountains, I pulled out my smartphone and ran a search for Thunderbears. There were more than I was expecting. Too many. More than you'd expect for a regular gathering, anyway. It made me believe without question that a specialized Thunderbear should be around there.

Though, despite the likelihood, there was no way to be certain. With the number of bears up here, the village was actually pretty lucky to only be slightly damaged. The damage to the farmer's fields wasn't as bad as it could've been, that was for sure. Plus, nobody had actually been attacked by a bear, either. The surrounding wilderness was probably full of small animals, berries, and nuts, so the Thunderbears didn't need to forage in civilized lands.

"Alrighty, let's get this over with..." I ran a target lock on all the Thunderbears in the area. But then I paused. The resources from the Thunderbears would go to waste if I killed them all with a mass spell.

Thunderbear pelt was quite valuable, as I recalled. Their liver was also an ingredient in a fast-acting and potent medication. Their meat was a little tough, but wasn't entirely awful either. If I burned them all up with a spell, I'd probably lose their pelts entirely. That wouldn't be economically intelligent of me.

I decided that the best way to kill them was with a bladed weapon, because stabbing them would damage the fur the least. Then I changed my mind, and decided it might be smarter to poison them, or perhaps suffocate them, or cause them to go into cardiac arrest. I didn't think my paralysis spell was strong enough to induce heart attacks, though.

"Confirm the number of Thunderbears in the region."

"Calculating... Twenty-three bears. Cubs included." Cubs or not, I couldn't afford mercy. Didn't want to run the risk of the little guys growing up and causing havoc. I felt slightly uncomfortable, but... that's life.

It'd probably be best to shoot them right in the hearts, one by one, huh... I figured it'd only take about an hour to end all of their lives. As I pondered the best way to effectively take them out, I popped open a portal to the first bear.

"Hrmph... That was quite the hassle..." The specialized Thunderbear was a lot tougher than I expected, and didn't really give me much room to attack it. I couldn't aim anywhere except for the heart, so I had to dodge a bunch of lightning bolts that fired at me from all angles. It was really tough to avoid, but I ended up defeating it in the end. I put it in [**Storage**] with the rest of the bear corpses.

And, just like that, the mountain was free of Thunderbears. Now all I had to do was head to the guild. Firstly, I needed to exchange the raw bear parts for money. And secondly, I had to inform them that the quest set by the town needed to be cancelled. Though, it probably wouldn't be a cancellation, since the quest likely hadn't even reached the guild board yet.

"Uhh... what was it called, again? Uhh... Right, Senka. The town of Senka." I looked it up on my map. It was due west.

I triggered my flight magic and began heading there immediately. Truly, it was among my most convenient of spells. If I was on the ground, I could probably reach the same speed with [**Accel Boost**], but this method was easier. That being said, [**Fly**] was slightly slower and didn't increase my thought processing in the way [**Accel**] did. Both spells had their pros and cons, it was just up to me to employ them at the right times.

As such idle thoughts rolled around my head, I eventually saw a town through a clearing of clouds. It was Senka.

I'd cause a fuss if I ended up landing in the middle of town, so I landed just a bit outside of the place. Then, after confirming the location of the guild on the map, I headed right into the bustling streets.

The guildhouse in Senka was considerably smaller than the one in Belfast's capital, but the interior was actually quite nice. The quest board, as usual, was up on a far wall with several jobs posted. I gave it a sidelong glance before heading to the reception desk.

"Welcome! How may I help you?"

"I'd like to sell some materials I've harvested from some monsters. Also, there'll be a quest coming in from Colette village tomorrow. I'd like to cancel it."

"I don't quite understand." The receptionist eyed me suspiciously, so I presented her my guild card and explained the situation. She was surprised to see a Silver Rank, but believed my story.

After that was dealt with, I lined up the Thunderbears outside and had them check the quality. I set aside two Thunderbear corpses to bring back to the village as evidence, as well.

"Th-This will take us a little while, is that alright?" I didn't mind, there were a lot. It was just one of those things, it'd be unreasonable to complain. I decided to kill time by looking around the guild. Making my way over to the quest board, I browsed a few requests.

"Hm… A Mega Slime… in a cave to the east, huh." All the girls in my party loathed any species even remotely similar to Slimes. I'd fought many a monster and demon since I came to the new world, but slippery slimy monsters like Ropers and Slimes were ones we rarely encountered.

As I idly browsed through jobs, someone came through the guild entrance. Many adventurers were coming and going, so I didn't think much of it, but… then I did a double-take.

"Well then, if it isn't Touya. What brings you here?"

"Ende…?!" It was him. The monochrome boy. With his pale complexion, his snow-white hair, his signature white scarf and his dark outfit…

"What are you doing here, Ende?"

"I should ask you the same, shouldn't I? I just got back from wiping out a King Ape that was rampaging in the area." Ende smiled wryly at me, and gave his answer. I knew what he was talking about. They were a large, monkey-like monster. They weren't very intelligent, that was for sure. At least the ones I'd fought hadn't been.

"No, those details aren't important. There's a lot I need to ask of you, Ende."

"You have something to ask me? I mean, go right ahead, but please give me a moment. I need to turn in the quest, after all." I watched Ende go to the reception desk and hand his guild card over. It was red. After pocketing his reward, we went to a corner area in the guild and sat down.

"What did you want from me, Touya?"

"The Phrase. I want to know what they are." Ende looked like he was deep in thought, but eventually started to talk.

"Regarding the Phrase... there are things I can tell you, and things I cannot tell you. Are you still fine with that?"

"...That's fine. Just tell me what you can." Ende leaned forward in his seat and began to talk to me.

"You may find this hard to believe, Touya. But the Phrase are not entities native to this world. It would be more appropriate to call them visitors that came to this world from another."

"Visitors? They're a little hostile for that, aren't they? Seem more like invaders to me."

"I don't think calling them invaders is quite apt. They have no invasive intentions. The only reason they're in this world is to find their leader."

The Sovereign Phrase. That's what Ende told me last time. That it was the goal of the Phrase to locate their leader.

"Then why are they killing people?!"

"...Please understand that from this point, there are details I'll have to exclude. The thing that keeps a Phrase alive is the core. So long as the Phrase Core is intact, the creature will not die, and it will slowly absorb residual magic from the atmosphere until it can eventually regenerate its body. The Phrase are here to find the Sovereign Core. Because that core is somewhere in this world. They're killing humans in an attempt to find and reclaim it."

"But that doesn't make sense. What does finding the Sovereign Core have to do with killing people?"

"The search is precisely why they're killing people. Because the Sovereign Core is inside the body of someone living in this world."

That sounded insane to me. The Sovereign Core was actually inside a person?

"It's not only limited to humans, either. It could dwell within a beastman, one of the demonkin, any creature with a reasonable degree of intelligence could be housing the Sovereign Core. It's currently in a dormant state. For all intents and purposes, it's in a state of near-death. While the Sovereign Core is dormant, it latches on to a lifeform's body and gestates within it, waiting for the next stage of its life cycle. The Phrase noticed the 'waves' being pulsed out by the dormant core, and that's why they know it's in this world. But they can't discern the exact position, because there are too many noises drowning the signal out. They can't hear the noise of the Sovereign properly over the sound of the beating of its host's heart. Therefore, they slaughter humans with reckless abandon, all in the name of clearing the obstructive noise."

If what he was saying was true, that was insane! The Phrase would just keep killing until they eventually plucked their leader from a corpse.

"Just what the hell are the Phrase?"

"Originally, they were beings that evolved and lived on another world. But, after some time, their leader disappeared. Since then, they've been traveling across worlds in pursuit of the Sovereign Core, in order to regain their leader. The Sovereign has its own intentions and agenda, as well. They're coarse, and unrefined creatures. Their methods are brutal, I know. But you have to understand, they aren't acting out of malice, but raw instinct."

The situation reminded me of bee and ant hives, and how the colony moved according to the Queen. They were definitely gathering here like something was attracting them. But I wondered what Ende meant when he said that the Sovereign had an agenda. "When the Sovereign Core crosses to a new world, it will infest the body of someone who lives there. Little by little, it will absorb the life force and magic from that person, and then warp into a new host when its previous one reaches the end of their life. This process repeats until the Sovereign Core has absorbed enough power to travel to another world."

"...So that's it? The Phrase come here seeking the Sovereign Core, killing indiscriminately in the process, and then they'll follow the core to the next world along after it leaves?"

"That's about the gist of it, yes." That was absolutely insane. I couldn't believe what I was hearing. They were like locusts moving from crop field to crop field, draining it of life. They recklessly traversed worlds, harvesting the people within and moving on. To make matters worse, they didn't even seem aware of their destruction. They were just doing it because it was their job. It wasn't even a case of good or evil to them. They were just running on instinct.

"...Ende, you said you were hunting for the Sovereign Core as well. Does that mean you've killed humans?"

"Don't be silly, now. I wouldn't want you to get the wrong impression. I'm simply waiting for the core to finish its cycle and transition to the next world, and then I'll follow. Don't lump me in with the monsters." Ende's intentions were completely confusing to me, I couldn't get a read on him at all. I wondered if he was perhaps some kind of guardian assigned to the Sovereign Core... That didn't change the fact that the Sovereign Core being here was the reason why everything was going wrong, though.

"What was that thing about the boundary of the world?"

"Hm... that's a bit of a stickler to explain. Let's try to think of it like a staircase. Each step is connected to the step immediately above and below it, right? You can take one step no problem, but going ten steps at a time isn't possible, right? You can consider the height between steps to be the gaps between worlds. In order to get ten steps higher, you have to go up all the steps between the one you're on and that ten-step goal... though you might be able to skip a step or two along the way. Worlds right next to each other have common features, but worlds far apart are vastly different. But that aside, usually there's a barrier in place that prevents beings from crossing to other worlds. So you shouldn't even be able to make a single step." I felt like I understood his explanation for the most part. There were common features between my world and the world I now lived in, so they probably weren't too many steps apart.

"I might've mentioned something like this, I don't remember... but the boundary is not like a wall. It's more of a translucent membrane. Small and harmless things generally go unregistered and can pass through freely. That is the reason why the Sovereign Core expends all of its reserved power to travel, letting it float through in its death-like dormant state. It's an ability only the Sovereign can make use of." That made sense enough to me, at least with the information I had. I wondered what it physically felt like, to pass through to another world in your own body…

"It shouldn't normally be possible to break through the boundary line, but… making a rip is possible, and an individual creature could force its way through. If that happens several times, eventually the rip will get bigger and bigger, until the boundary falls and can no longer do its job, allowing anything to spill out. That's what happened five thousand years ago." That was the Phrase Invasion that Doctor Babylon had told me about. She said the world was on the verge of destruction… Now it all made sense.

"Back then, the boundary line was somehow repaired, and the threat of the Phrase vanished. The remaining Phrase were all vanquished, and this world was spared the fate of many others. I also aided in hunting the remnants." It was then that I knew Ende was not human. He was absolutely not an ordinary person, and he spoke so lightly and familiarly of events that transpired five thousand years ago.

But his words made me wonder just what it was that had restored the boundary line, it seemed Ende wasn't sure either, and that made me all the more curious.

"I thought I'd be able to take it easy a while, but things started getting noisy again. The boundary line barrier is starting to come unfurled again. It's barely holding, but it'll only be a matter of time before the high-tier Phrase break through it. I can't tell you if that'll happen in a year or fifty years, though…"

"Ende… are you an ally or an enemy of humanity?"

"Hm… I wonder about that one. I've been hunting the Phrase, but it's been more of a way to kill time than anything else. If the boundary breaks down, I might sit it out and let nature take its course. That being said, I don't much feel like being an ally of the

Phrase." I couldn't understand Ende's intentions at all, much less his motivations. I decided to let it go, because at the very least he wasn't sleeping with the enemy.

"I have something I need to take care of, now. Can we consider our chat concluded?" Ende stood up and made for the exit.

"…Just one last question. Ende, who or what are you?"

"Me? You can just call me a 'drifter.' See you around, Touya." Ende walked out of the guild, leaving me only with those words.

The Phrase's mission, the Sovereign Core… the Boundary Line…

I learned a lot of crazy stuff from Ende that day. When the reality of the situation set in, I realized that things were actually pretty dire. Five thousand years ago, the crisis was averted because the boundary barrier was repaired… But what about this time? Could the Phrase even be stopped? They were clearly going to kill humans indiscriminately in their search for the Sovereign Core. It's not like this world had much in the way of opposition for them, either. We didn't have any of the advanced technology that the world had back then, so if they appeared in waves we'd be completely screwed.

As these uncertain, uncomfortable truths milled around in my head, I received my money from the receptionist and left the guild.

"And that's the situation. Do you know much about it?"

"No, I cannot say that I do. As I said earlier, I am not always keeping an eye on all places. But there are indeed races that travel across worlds. Naturally I do not interfere with those species, either. Though, it would be another story entirely if another God was causing trouble or something…" On my way back from talking to Ende, I tried calling up God to ask about what I'd discovered. But, as I'd expected, he didn't really know anything at all. As usual, the people of this world would have to solve their own issues.

The situation was by no means dire just yet, but I knew that I'd have to start making preparations should the worst come to pass.

I reasoned that the most efficient way to deal with the issue would be using the power of Babylon. Doctor Babylon had prepared a final weapon, the Frame Gear, for the final clash against the Phrase. I had a feeling that the weapon would be necessary if I wanted to repel their resurgence.

That course of action left me with two methods. I had to either procure the blueprints from the storehouse, or the product itself from the Hangar.

As I recalled, the parts of Babylon remaining were the hangar, the library, the storehouse, the rampart, the tower, and the research laboratory. I had a one in three chance of getting the one I wanted if I found them at random.

"I should probably start picking up the pace of my search, huh…" I flew back to Colette village as I pondered my next course.

"A Frame Gear, sir?" After returning from the village, I immediately went up to the workshop to talk with Rosetta. The Doctor had created the Frame Gear, so I was certain that Rosetta had to at least be slightly familiar with it.

"Yeah, how do they work exactly?"

"Just about anyone can operate it, sir! The proficiency is determined by both the pilot's magical affinity, and their personal affinity for the Frame Gear model, sir! That being said, it'd be a challenge to get it to move very well without any training, yessir!"

Makes sense... That means if I can mass-produce them, we'd definitely be looking good. I mean, she raises a fair point about the individual skill of the pilots, but... we'd definitely be able to repel the Phrase if we had a giant robot army to oppose them.

"Mass production of the Frame Gears would prove difficult, sir!"

"Huh? Why's that? Can't we just copy it in the workshop?"

"The amount of materials needed is pretty crazy, I won't lie. On top of that, creating a single, very basic model Frame Gear in the workshop would take an entire day at least."

That sucks... A whole day for one robot? That's only thirty Frame Gears in a month. I mean, thirty giant robots is definitely a lot, don't get me wrong, but... According to the Doctor, there were like tens of thousands of Phrase during the attack back then! I don't feel so good all of a sudden...

"How many robots were in the Hangar when you lost contact?"

"Let me think... I must confess, sir. I was not involved with the other Babylons as much as my own. But, as far as I understand it, there should be seven completed Frame Gear models within the Hangar."

"Seven, seriously? How did they plan on taking out the Phrase with so few...?"

"We were about to begin mass production of the Frame Gears, sir... but the Phrase vanished just as soon as we had drawn up plans to build a second and third workshop." Rosetta spoke up, disappointment evident in her voice.

Huh, so there were plans to make the workshop bigger? Well, that at least explains why there aren't many Frame Gears. The crisis resolved itself entirely before they even had a chance to start responding properly.

All I could do in the meantime was gather the necessary materials. As I exited the workshop, Cesca and Flora came walking over from the alchemy lab. The two of them carried a basket that held several medicine bottles.

"What's that, medicine?"

"Uhuhu... these are some general-use medicines for colds, headaches, stomach aches, and other common ailments, see? There wasn't much in the way of medication in the castle, so I whipped up a batch, you see?" Flora, still clad in her nurse outfit, answered cheerily.

I'm still not used to seeing this kinda thing outside of a hospital...

So she was making medicine. Even with my restorative magic and utilities like [**Recovery**], there was still stuff I couldn't quite relieve.

Wait a second...

"Flora, do you need the alchemy lab to make medicine?"

"Heavens no. This is just regular medicine, you see? I don't need such complex facilities for this. I used the facilities here to refine them and increase their potency, see? I can still make them the regular way, but they'd be less effective and it would just take me a little longer." That meant other people should be able to make use of the alchemy lab facilities too... If we could produce medicine, then that was another export we'd be able to use for trade.

Headaches, digestive problems, sinus blockages... these kinds of issues affected people the world over. Selling remedies probably wouldn't make us obscenely rich, but it would definitely help us rake in some extra income. I decided that we should dedicate some resources to harvesting the raw materials for the medicine, so that they could be refined within Babylon.

I told Flora my idea, and then instructed her to teach some of Tsubaki's subordinates about how to refine the ingredients and make the superior medicine. They were ninjas, so they obviously would've had a basic medicinal knowledge already, so I picked out the most medically inclined of them and assigned them to the alchemy lab. With that, we were ready to begin mass production of refined medicines.

I headed back to the castle with Cesca and Flora, and immediately went to see Leen so I could consult with her about what Ende had told me.

If we wanted to get technical, Leen was only the ambassador to my country from Mismede, but I considered the Phrase to be an issue that transcended national borders.

"...So there's a Sovereign Phrase... an invasion from another world... and a world boundary, you say?" Leen sat back in her chair, letting a heavy sigh escape her mouth. She was clearly surprised. Paula stood next to her, arms folded.

"I've lived a very long time indeed, but this is the first I've heard of such things... Usually I would ask you to stop joking around, but... the evidence here is overwhelming, so I'll unhappily concede that you're telling the truth."

"Well, there's always the possibility that Ende fed me a bunch of lies. I'm still trying to figure out if that's the case."

"Regardless, there'll be people that won't believe it even if it is true... Right up until the Phrase begin tearing their families apart, that is."

She was right. There'd definitely be some who, even if they acknowledged that the Phrase existed, would only view them as a new species of monster. We'd only met three types, after all. The Cricket Phrase in the ancient ruins, the Manta Phrase in the Rabbi

Desert, and the Spider Phrase in the Sea of Trees... Ah, there was also the snake one that Leen and the soldiers had encountered in Mismede.

It was possible that there were more Phrase in the world that Ende had killed already, though.

If we sat around twiddling our thumbs then we'd be dead the moment the boundary failed. We'd need to make preparations before it was too late.

Those preparations currently hinged on searching for the remaining Babylon pieces, and collecting the raw materials required to build a Frame Gear.

"We've been trying to find information on ancient ruins, that much is sure. Please allocate more resources to the hunt. I've found many structures, but most of them are just abandoned buildings without anything of note within them. It's somewhat disheartening to constantly fail, understand?" *Whoops... right... in the end, only Leen's subordinates had been sent out to look. I should probably actually send some guys out to do that too.*

After bidding goodbye to Leen, I went to visit Kohaku and the other beasts to ask if there'd be a creature suited to summon for scouting operations.

"If you assk me, it ssshould be the oness that fly up in the sssky, no? They're very fassst, and can go to a great many placess." Kokuyou made an interesting proposal. I hadn't considered summoning birds for the hunt, but they were definitely versatile enough.

"Master, it would take quite some time to contract with each and every bird individually. Might I recommend forging a pact with the one that governs the entire race instead?"

"Hm. Sango... You're proposing our liege summon *that* one?" Kohaku cut in on Sango's speech. I wondered just what they were referring to. "The Flame Monarch. The same as us, a monarch with wings. One that controls fire. If you summoned and successfully contracted with the Flame Monarch, you'd have thousands of birds immediately at your disposal."

I see... Kohaku's the leader of the beasts, Kokuyou and Sango collectively lead reptilian creatures... They can summon and control monsters of this type without any real problem, and generally make use of them. That power is mine by extension. Though the control doesn't stretch to magical beasts like Thunderbears or King Apes.

So basically, it's the bird version of that.

"What kind of person is the Flame Monarch?"

"Despite their moniker of roaring fires, the Flame Monarch is kind and calm. Of us, they are the one with the noblest character." Kohaku began to speak well of the bird, but Kokuyou suddenly butted in with a sly grin.

"Are you ssssure? I'm fairly certain that I'm the one with the bessst perssonality here, sweetie."

"Be silent. You're quicker to boil than a pot."

"You take that back, bitch!" Just like that, Kokuyou was brought to boil. What an apt comparison.

After the two of them calmed down, I decided to call upon the Flame Emperor.

I drew up the summoning circle in the courtyard and began to focus my Dark magic. Eventually, a black mist began to form in the air around us. Kohaku and the others began to channel their own magic into the fog. I focused my magic even further, and the misty fog became thicker.

"Thee who governs the scalding summers, and the roaring flames. Thee who governs the shores of lakes, and the southern winds. I implore you, present yourself before me." The fog began to swell with tremendous magical power, and a cylinder of roaring fire emerged from the magic circle. The vortex blew all the fog away, and eventually dispersed to reveal a huge, red bird.

It was about the size of a horse. It looked almost identical to what I could only describe as a Phoenix. This was the Flame Emperor.

"Ah, it's you fellows. How nostalgic, it has been some time."

"Indeed it has, Flame Emperor."

"Long time no sssee, flamey baby."

"A flashy entrance as ever, Flame Emperor." The Flame Emperor's voice sounded a bit like a gentle young woman's. She definitely seemed calm and regal, without being aloof. Kohaku might've been right about her.

"Was it you that summoned me, boy?"

"That's right."

"This man is our lord, Mochizuki Touya." The Flame Emperor made an expression that I assumed was bird for 'surprised.' But, after some time spent gazing at me, she closed her eyes.

"So be it. As the master of the White Monarch, and the master of the Black Monarch, I know now that you will likely qualify for any challenge I give you. Let us make a contract. I will become subordinate to you, there is no need to test you, for you have already passed. Mochizuki Touya, my liege… grant unto me a name."

What…? That sure went smooth. She doesn't want anything from me? That's a first. But I'm definitely not gonna complain about it. Kohaku was right about you, lady… you're the best of the lot as far as character goes.

I still had to think of a name, though. I had Kohaku, Sango, and Kokuyou, and they were all named after precious stones, so… I knew what I had to do.

"Kougyoku. That's the name I've chosen for you. It means Ruby, a crimson stone. How about it?"

"Kougyoku… I'll readily accept it, then. From hereon, that is my name." With a poof, the Flame Emperor transformed herself into a small bird, around the size of a parrot, and landed on my shoulder. That size was much more agreeable to me. She wasn't likely to cause chaos as a tiny bird.

At any rate, I decided to actually do what I had set out to do to begin with.

I loaned Kougyoku's power and summoned about a thousand birds at the same time. They were all different size and species, but I sent them all off to the four corners of the sky regardless.

I telepathically ordered them all to inform me if they came across any suspicious-looking ruins, monuments, or facilities. I hoped from the bottom of my heart that they'd find something, and fast.

It was all up to them at that point, all I had left was my hope.

Some time had passed since I'd sent out my avian scouts, but none had reported back with anything of note. The boundary of the world was on the verge of tearing, and there was nothing I could do…

Even though God managed the worlds, he definitely had it rough. I hated that some people had the audacity to blame him for being inattentive. If you have a big collection of books and a bug starts eating through one of the pages of one of them, how would you know until you checked again? It's not like he could keep an eye on a specific page just in case there might've been a bug nibbling at it.

"Can't you use your search magic to look for that Sovereign Core, Touya?" Once again I sighed toward Elze.

"How many times do I have to tell you? I can't find something that I haven't seen, especially not if I only have a vague grasp on what it actually is. If I even knew its shape or size or something it might help me form a mental image, but it's inside a human to begin with, so there's no way of me working that out." My search spell definitely wasn't accurate. It depended on my subjective criteria, after all. Let's say there were two people in front of me. If one was a woman, and the other was a man who had used magic to disguise himself perfectly as a woman, the search spell would still list him as a woman.

If it was a guy who had poorly disguised himself as a woman, it would judge him as a man, though, because that's what I'd see him as. That being said, it would sometimes slip up and judge a woman as a man if she had a particularly strong jawline or mannish features...

In other words, it only searched by my own standards. Also, a strong enough magical barrier could negate it. I could search for things that were "similar," but... How would I even know what was similar to the Sovereign Core to begin with if I have no initial frame of reference? If I walked over to a rock and asserted to myself, "This is the Sovereign Core," then I'd probably get results for that term all over the world wherever there were rocks like that one.

"At any rate, it's not like I can take care of it that easily." I muttered quietly as I used my reshaping spell in the middle of the

217

training grounds. It's not like I could do anything, so there was no point moping. Instead, I focused on reshaping the leather in my hands.

"Milord, what's this?" Before I'd noticed him there, Logan was talking to me. He had a wooden training sword in one hand, and was wiping his face with the towel he held in the other. He was, of course, referring to what I held in my hand.

"This is a glove, Logan. I was thinking of teaching the children in the town how to play baseball."

"A... glove?"

"For catching, I mean... bah, here, I'll just show you instead." I took out a ball I'd made earlier, threw it against the castle wall, then caught it in my glove when it bounced back. I hadn't worn a baseball glove since I was in elementary school, but the feeling still... fit like a glove.

"This is how you play, see? You gotta catch the ball. Usually the game has nine players facing off against another nine, though."

"Huh..." I made another glove and gave it to Logan. We tried to play a basic game of catch. He missed the first few times, but quickly got the hang of it. I'd noticed it a few times, but the people of this world were definitely quick on the uptake.

The other soldiers started looking at us with envious eyes as they finished up their training. Sensing that, I had the ball and glove copied in the workshop and the copies were distributed to everyone. Vice-Commander Nikola smiled wryly, but their training was done for the day so he couldn't do anything. I still felt a little sorry, for some reason.

I started counting up the amount of people there were. We had enough for baseball, so I decided to ask if they wanted to play. They might even end up finding it fun, I hoped.

I took everyone who had free time along with me, and I created a baseball field to the west of the castle. I constructed the bases, a batter box, and a pitcher mound.

I crafted new bats, mitts, and protectors for everyone, then taught everyone the basic rules of baseball. I didn't actually know the rules that thoroughly, though, so I made a point to consult the final details on my smartphone later.

For the time being, I decided just to wing it and take the position of referee. The game finally began, and I watched them go at it.

To be blunt, it went terribly for the most part. There were a ton of strikeouts and dead balls. Nobody ran properly, and ended up walking to the bases. But, gradually, they began to get the hang of it. They started hitting the ball properly with the bat. They were finally displaying the finesse I'd have expected from experienced swordsmen. And, as the offense grew, the defensive players began to shine as well.

They kept screwing up to begin with, sure. There was a lot of fumbling around and falling. But, through trial and error, they gradually improved their form. I was pretty surprised by how well they ended up doing, but then I remembered these men were all soldiers at near-peak physical fitness levels. These guys were very proficient athletes.

I popped open a portal and called the children from the town over. I'd decided that the soldiers had begun playing well enough to deserve a proper audience. I briefed them on the rules as I made some spectator stands for them to sit in.

"You hit it, go for it!!

"Run!"

"Do your best, team!" The kids got into the spirit of the game and began yelling and cheering. The Knights began to cheer on their respective teams with newfound vigor.

"What're you doing, dumbass?! Throw it to first base!"

"Look up at the ball, put your hand up!"

"Switch places, switch with me!!" The knights, for the most part, were actually jeering at the enemy teams. I wished they were a bit more childishly innocent, like the kids.

I didn't really go into the rules too deeply, so people started making blunders here and there that I wasn't entirely certain about. I had to learn more about it later.

"Well, just so long as they're having fun..." As everyone got absorbed in the action, I started finishing up the stadium. I finished an outfield fence, a scoreboard, and a net to catch any stray balls. I was quite proud of it, when all was done.

It was getting dark, so it was about time to call it a night. I left the baseball equipment with the knight order and told them they were free to play in the stadium when they had time to kill. As for the kids, I made smaller equipment for them to play with when they visited. I didn't make any special facility for them, or anything. There was more than enough land for them to play amateur baseball on.

The next day, off-duty knights began making frequent trips to the stadium in order to play. They'd already split off into several teams, from the looks of things. They were even setting up little leagues. Their teams had the names of monsters, like "The Griffins" and "The Salamanders," which made me think that the people of this world really weren't all too different from the people of mine.

Whenever there was an issue with the rules, people would come and consult me about it. But every time they did that, I had to look it up on the internet. I decided to cut out the middleman and just make a rulebook, but there were a few problems.

I could use one of my spells to transcribe the text into paper, but that also left the issue of converting Japanese into this world's language. Not to mention the fact that I'd need to sift through everything to remove confusing words like "America" or "Major League," I didn't want people getting really muddled.

Eventually, as the regular townsfolk began showing an interest in baseball as well, they all started to come up and watch the games be played. Some of them started joining in after a while as well. And, sensing the opportunity to make a pretty penny, the Mismedian merchant, Olba, negotiated with me for the sales rights to baseballs and baseball accessories.

I agreed to the deal, since I didn't really see a reason to decline. He would produce them elsewhere, and a percentage of the profits would make their way back to my country. It was very much a similar deal to the one we'd made about the spinning tops. Back then I wasn't sure about the widespread appeal, but the spinning tops had become a hit with kids in several nations, so it was possible I was about to begin a baseball craze too.

At the monthly alliance meeting with the other western national leaders, the loud cheering from the stadium caught the attention of the emperors and kings. The moment I showed them the source of the excitement, they fell head over heels for baseball.

I offered each national leader a set of baseball equipment, though it was more fair to say that they all bothered me for some. Each country created a national baseball team. And, just like clockwork, the game became very popular. Baseball as a sport became a casual activity in almost every developed nation. Who could've seen that one coming?

When people had free time, they'd band together with their friends and form teams, and then they'd play against other teams. Their family members and other friends would watch them play. It seemed like cheerleading was starting to naturally catch on as a consequence as well... It didn't look like professional baseball leagues were far off, if I was honest.

I never quite expected it to blow up to the extent that it did, but Olba told me it was his intention and anticipation from the beginning.

"I had no idea it'd be this successful..."

"Your Highness, it's something you began, so naturally it would be a smash hit. If you'll pardon the joke." Olba answered me with a small chuckle. He was right. I'd completely forgotten how devoid of entertainment this world was. There wasn't really much variety in general life, let alone sports. That was honestly a little sad, if you asked me. It made me wonder if I'd be able to sell anything if I marketed it as a "fun game."

"Now then, if you have yourself any other bright ideas... please do not hesitate to ask my company for assistance in sales and distribution..."

"Mm, well, I actually have a lot of ideas right now. But I'm not sure if they'll all sell..."

"Ohoho... How very interesting..." I saw a devious glint in Olba's eyes just then. That was probably his senses as a trader. I decided to make use of that keen eye.

"But, that aside for a minute... I'm going to need metals. Copper, iron, silver, mithril, orichalcum, and hihi'irokane... Can you use your trade connections to get these at decent prices?"

"Metals, eh? Well, I think there's a particular trader who can get me these on the cheap, yes. How much do you need?"

"I need them indefinitely, for now at least. From now on, please use my cut of the profits from any inventions I give you to purchase these materials for me." I decided to start preparing well in advance for the Frame Gear, that way even if it needed a ton of materials it shouldn't be a problem. I decided to start stockpiling. I wasn't sure I'd be able to get enough materials to make a Frame Gear if I only focused on gathering materials alone.

"It seems you must have a sufficient reason, then... I'll begin searching for the relevant materials. Color me intrigued."

"Thanks for your understanding. So then, on to the goods. They're called the yo-yo, the hula-hoop, the hopscotch, and the ball-and-cup."

"I've never heard of these before. Can you tell me more?" I made a yo-yo and tried to use it in order to show Olba how it was. The plastic types were the best, but I had to make one out of wood. I ended up crafting the other toys too, and demonstrated them all to him one by one.

With that, I'd secured the funds to acquire materials for the Frame Gear. I felt a little bit awkward using sales proceeds of other people to fuel my project, though. I decided to kill a Mithril Golem later on to make myself feel better, it probably wouldn't be much of a challenge compared to the first time I went up against one, though...

At any rate, things were starting to look up.

"Congratulations!"

"Congratulations, you two! I wish you all the best!"

"You better not make your new wife cry, Lyon!"

"May you two be blessed with happiness!" Celebratory clapping filled the air. In the center of all the noise stood Lyon, a knight of Belfast. A little embarrassed, he beamed happily, standing next to his former fiancee. Indeed, she was now his wife. His wife was Olga, a foxgirl.

Lyon was bedecked in a splendid snow-colored tuxedo, while Olga wore a pure white wedding dress.

I had designed both of their outfits using references I had found online. Then I'd asked Zanac, the clothing merchant, to sew them. The two both had great figures, so they filled out the clothes nicely. I was honestly a little jealous.

The wedding was being held at Lyon's parents' house... in other words, General Leon's villa. More specifically, in the Blitz estate's courtyard.

The bride and groom's families, all of Lyon's fellow knights, and their friends from Mismede had all gathered to see them wed.

I'd opened up a portal to invite the Mismede guests over. Well, I suppose this could be called a success.

The newlyweds' new home was within walking distance of the wedding venue. It was a nice house, but a bit too small to hold a grand affair like this. Which is why the wedding was being held at the groom's parents' villa.

The party was held buffet style in the courtyard. I'd attended their wedding not as the grand duke of Brunhild, but as the couple's friend.

With me was Yumina, Elze, Linze, Yae, and Lu. Lu didn't really know either the bride or the groom, but I didn't want her to feel left out, so I brought her along too.

The guests all chatted amicably with each other. One of them broke off from the crowd and headed toward me.

"Your Highness, I humbly thank you for everything you've done for the bride and groom."

"Don't mention it. Besides, I'm here today not as a Duke, but as their friend."

The grey-suited gentleman bowing to me was Olba, the merchant. He was Olga's father. His build was as sturdy as always, and his fox ears and tail were twitching slightly.

But what caught my attention were the two women standing behind Olba. They were both foxgirls, and they looked to be in their late thirties. Though she had golden hair instead of silver, one of the ladies resembled Olga. Was she maybe…?

As I shifted my gaze over to them, Olba beckoned them forward.

"Ah, let me introduce you to my family. Arisa, Irma, this is the grand duke of Brunhild."

"I am Olba Strand's wife, Arisa Strand. It is a pleasure to make your acquaintance, Your Highness."

"Similarly, I am his wife, Irma Strand. Thank you so much for everything you've done for our daughter."

So they were Olba's wives. I was surprised to find out that he had two, though!

"Irma is the mother of Olga and Arma. Arisa is the mother of my eldest son, Ikusa." So the golden-haired Irma was the mother of Olga and Arma. No wonder they looked so similar.

Meanwhile, Arisa was the mother of Olga's older brother. Said older brother was apparently studying commerce in Roadmare, and hadn't been able to make it to the wedding.

"So you had two wives, huh?"

"Hahaha. I'd say that's not too many, really. Many of my merchant acquaintances have as many as five wives and eight mistresses, you know." Polygamy seemed to be completely fine in Mismede. Though it seemed the wives were ranked in a hierarchy.

It seemed polygamy was acceptable in Belfast as well, as long as you held a rank of baron or higher. Of course mistresses didn't count, so even if you were a commoner you could keep plenty so long as you had the funds to support them. Which meant you had to be a wealthy merchant, basically.

Incidentally, although Lyon's father was a baron, since he was the second son, he wouldn't get to inherit the title. So Olga would be his only wife.

He could still keep mistresses, but knowing him, I doubt he would. He was head over heels for Olga.

"Now that I think about it, if you hadn't helped set the two of them up, this might never have happened. You have my thanks for giving us ties to such an influential family as well." Olba spoke earnestly as he watched his daughter and son-in-law happily entertain a crowd of friends. Behind Olga stood her younger sister, Arma, carrying a flower basket. Arma looked happy as well.

"Oh yes, I almost forgot. For their wedding present, I constructed a hot spring inside their house. Once the ceremony's over, you should give it a try. It draws its water from a source in Belfast, and it does wonders for exhaustion."

"Hoho… a hot spring you say?"

"My, how wonderful!"

"Let's have a little soak on our way back, dear!"

Olba's wives seemed more excited about the spring than he did. Even a rich family didn't have many opportunities to enjoy hot springs. Doubly so for one from Mismede.

As Olba was the bride's father, he still had to go around and formally greet all of the other guests. After a few more minutes of talking he took his leave and started going around the courtyard.

"He looked really happy."

"It's his daughter's wedding, why wouldn't he be happy?"

As I replied to Yumina I mused on how things might have been different if Olga's parents had been less willing to let her go.

I'd like to think I wouldn't become the kind of father that goes on about how they'd never let anyone have their daughter, but who knows. I wasn't confident that I wouldn't be too doting.

Oh, looks like it's the groom's parents coming over this time.

"Hey Sir Tou… my apologies, it's Your Highness now, isn't it? Anyway, thank you for all that you've done for our foolish son." Lyon's father, General Leon, humbly bowed his head to me.

"Oh please, don't. I'm here as a friend, you can just talk to me like you always have."

"Is that so? Then I'll take you up on that offer, but just for today. I never dreamed you would rise up to the position of royalty. Ah, but if you'd married the princess, you could have become the King of Belfast too. I suppose regardless of your decision, it was always possible you'd be a leader."

It's true that was always a possibility, but the situation had changed a lot now.

I had my own country to run, and though I hadn't made it public yet, I was engaged to Yumina.

And since it seemed Belfast's queen had hidden herself from the public eye for some time, it was very possible that a proper successor would be born soon.

If a son was born, they wouldn't need me. But, if the new child was a girl, any guys Yumina gives birth to would become the heir to Belfast. Which would make any son born from the other four girls the heir to Brunhild.

There was a mountain of problems I still needed to think about. I hadn't even gotten married yet. I really shouldn't be worried about kids.

"Father! You can't speak so casually to the ruler of a country..." I heard a reproachful voice from behind the general. I turned to see a tall man in his late twenties sporting the same moustache as Leon. I felt like the only non-moustached guy in the world. But if he called Leon his father, then he must have been...

"Oh yes, this would be your first time meeting him, Lord Touya. This is Shyon, Lyon's older brother. He's a member of the army's first division. Even though he's more skilled with the sword, he's a pathetic fellow who let his younger brother get married before him."

"Will you give that a rest already?! ...It's a pleasure to make your acquaintance, Your Highness, the Grand Duke of Brunhild. My name is Shyon Blitz, a soldier in the army's first division. Thank you so much for attending my little brother's wedding ceremony."

Shyon then bowed to Yumina, who was technically his boss; Lu, the princess of Regulus; and even to Elze and the others. It was obvious he shared his brother's straight-laced attitude. Or rather, they'd both inherited it from their father.

"I can't wait to see what my grandkids will look like. If I get a grandson, I'm going to train him myself. Imagine what someone with beast blood in them could do with my Fire Fist technique. He'd become the best martial artist in Belfast for sure!" *Hey old man, rein it in before you turn from a doting parent to a doting grandparent.* I wondered if the family would end up being alright.

Though it was true that their children would have beast blood in them and therefore be stronger than regular humans... I get the feeling even if their first child was a girl, General Leon would still try to teach her martial arts.

"Oh yes, didn't you establish a knight order in Brunhild as well? Next time you have the opportunity, why don't we do a joint training session with our knights and yours? I'm sure it'll be good practice for both sides."

"Yeah, that sounds like a good idea. My units are still new to being knights, so they're not very good at coordinating their movements yet. Though I'd say their individual strengths are pretty high."

"Hmm, it's true just strength isn't enough. But coordination between troops isn't something that can be forged in a day. You'll need a lot of training for that... Have you tried group drills?"

"You have a point... Maybe I should have more large-scale mock battles. They may end up having to fight large bandit groups or the like, so..."

"Hey, you two. Do you think you could talk about politics some other time? You do realize this is a wedding, right?"

Yumina interrupted our conversation. She looked rather fed up with us. Though her annoyance was definitely justified. We probably shouldn't have been talking about fighting and death during a wedding. It soured the mood…

"A-Anyway, I'll contact you about the details later."

"V-Very well. That seems wise. Now then, Your Highness. We'll be taking our leave."

General Leon and Shyon awkwardly hurried away from us and went over to the knights' table.

"Being enthusiastic about your work is a good thing, but could you forget about it while we're here at least?"

"Sorry, the conversation just sort of went in that direction. Plus his idea was interesting, so, you know…" Being scolded by Lu, of all people, I couldn't help but let a reluctant smile coat my face.

"I thought it was a pretty good suggestion, to be honest. Joint training sounds like it'd be a blast."

"To tell the truth, I also thought the same, I did." Elze and Yae spoke their opinions bluntly with reluctant smiles of their own, whilst exchanging glances with each other. Well, these two were just that type of people, really.

"Touya, shouldn't you be making preparations for your speech? It's scheduled for pretty soon, isn't it?" Linze reminded me of my next role. I'd almost totally forgotten about it. Since I was the grand duke of an entire country — small as it was — that technically made me the most important person in attendance. Because of that, I'd been asked to give a speech for the newly married couple.

Due to the fact that I was still somewhat unfamiliar with this world's customs, I had asked Kousaka to prepare a standard celebratory speech for the wedding on a paper script, but…

When I checked my coat's inner pocket, the only thing there was my good old reliable smartphone.

I checked my other pockets for the script containing the speech, alas... Even after checking my coat's outer pocket, the pocket in my pants, and the inside of my [Storage] spell, the paper containing the speech was nowhere to be found...

Eh? Huh? What in the...?

"...What's the matter?"

"...I think I've lost the paper with my speech on it..."

"What?!" The girls all yelled in unison.

Eh? Huh?! Did I accidentally drop it somewhere?! H-Hang on a minute! Without that script, I'm in some seriously deep shit! I can only remember bits and pieces of it, and that's hardly gonna help me here!

"Touya, sis says everyone's in place, and they're all waiting for you to stand up on the platform to give your speech!" Arma came up to me and greeted me with a smile as bright as the sun. All I could do was respond with a stiff, forced smile and reply with "I. Will. Be. Right. There."

"Touya, just remember! All you need to do is congratulate them! Give them words that celebrate the occasion! That's all they want from you!"

"Y-Yeah, you're right."

"You absolutely cannot say anything about 'growing apart from each other,' 'a ravine growing between people,' or 'how all things eventually come to an end.' Don't mention anything such as that which may invite misfortune! You understand what I am saying, do you not?!"

"Huh? Ah, I get it. Yeah, you're right. I'll keep that advice in mind."

This is bad. Very bad. At this rate I'm likely to fumble my words and say things I probably really shouldn't... Though at the same time, I can't exactly just stand up and say "Congratulations to the bride and

groom! Lyon, Olga, I wish you happiness in your new married life!"
because that feels way too impersonal...

It's not like I could just say nothing, either. That'd be too rude!
What was the standard practice for a wedding celebration? Should
I break out into song like somebody's uncle who showed up out of
nowhere but everyone loves anyway? No, no, no. Rejected. I'd be way
too embarrassed to do something like that. What else is there...?

"Oh yeah." In that moment, I had a flash of brilliance. In my
old world, there was a little something special of a standard tradition
for weddings. Normally I wouldn't be able to do that kind of thing
myself, but luckily for me I had *That Magic* to help me out here.

"Sorry, Arma. Can you ask them to wait for just ten more
minutes? I need time to make certain preparations, you see."

"Eh? Umm, well, okay. I'll ask them to wait a little longer." Arma
left in a dash heading back to the others.

Alright, time to get this show on the road.

I began my search for certain people whom I was sure would be
amongst the crowd for this occasion.

"Ahem. I stand here today as Mochizuki Touya, the grand
duke of Brunhild. To Lyon and Olga, I wish you all the best in your
marriage on this day." I made use of my Null spell, [**Speaker**], I made
sure that my voice would reach all those present in the garden. There
appeared to be some commotion among some guests present who
were unaware of my position as the grand duke of a country, but I
continued my speech in spite of that.

"From now on, these two will be building a family of their own.
For this joyous occasion, I would like to present to you the image of
a wonderful family that they may one day become themselves." Lyon
and Olga looked at each other, seeming puzzled by my words.

Keeping my eyes on them, I stepped down from the platform and cast my Null spell [**Mirage**].

What appeared upon the stage was the image of a young, yet great man. He was holding a newborn baby aloft, letting out a yell of joy. By his side was a woman smiling softly in joy, along with a young boy standing beside them.

The baby held aloft by the young man was letting out innocent, joyous laughter.

"…That's me."

"Eh?" Lyon let out a quiet whisper, which Olga overheard.

"…That baby is me, when I was just born. My brother… and my late mother, they're both there. The one holding me is my father, back when he was still young…" Lyon shifted his gaze over to his father, General Leon. Leon himself was looking straight ahead, entranced by the image before him.

The scene being displayed abruptly changed to a new scenario. This time there was a slim, fox-eared young man gazing lovingly into a cradle with a sleeping baby in it.

"Father…?" The young Olba gently poked the cheeks of the baby, and a gentle smile rose to his face. Irma, in the bed nearby, giggled at the sight.

Olba and Irma were likewise both captivated by the image before them.

Though the image itself was an illusion, the events themselves reflected actual events from the past. Just earlier, I had talked to General Leon, Shyon, Olba, Irma, Arisa, and two of their acquaintances, and requested that they let me see all of what they remembered of these events through my [**Recall**] spell. I then used those memories to recreate the image being projected upon the stage.

233

The significant events of the lives of the two young versions of Lyon and Olga began to play out one after another before the audience, accompanied by some fitting music.

The fact that Lyon was born with a weak body. The first time that he unwillingly took up sword training. The time he went fishing with his older brother. The time he got into a huge argument with his father. The time when his mother passed away. The time he persuaded his father to let him become a Royal Knight instead of a soldier in the standing army. The extremely strict training he undertook and overcame, becoming a splendid member of the knight order...

The fact that Olga was a tomboy as a child. The time she returned home late and was scolded by her mother for it. The time that she was overjoyed when her father brought back souvenirs from a far-off country. The time when her younger sister was born. The time when their whole family went on a trip together. The time that Olga studied and studied and did all that she could, before being accepted into the service of the palace. The time her family held a congratulatory party for her after being accepted into the palace...

The reflected memories of both families softly faded away, leaving behind an image of both Lyon and Olga as they were today. An image of the two smiling happily together, and both of their families congratulating them on the event.

And thus, the illusion softly and slowly faded out now that the story was over.

I stepped up onto the stage once more, and spoke to the two through my [Speaker].

"I hope that the love your families both poured their hearts into raising you will be passed on to you both, so that your children might grow up in a similarly wonderful family household. I believe, from the bottom of my heart, that the two of you will do this without my needing to tell you. I would like to present only words of celebration on this wonderful occasion to the both of you. With this, I end my speech in honor of the married couple. I wish you all the best in your new life together." Having finished my speech, I gave a bow. Everyone gathered immediately broke out into applause at my presentation. It made me feel pretty embarrassed.

I shifted my gaze to the bride and groom to find that both of them had broken down into tears. I wondered if maybe I'd overdone it a bit... Olga was hugging her mother, Irma, crying in her arms.

As I stepped down from the stage, Olba and General Leon both stood forward and bowed before me.

"You have my heartfelt gratitude for giving such a wonderful gift to us all."

"Likewise, my thanks to you, Touya. You've given us the greatest words of celebration that anyone ever could have." I had mixed feelings about the situation. I couldn't really tell them that I'd lost the actual script that had been prepared for me, and that I came up with this idea on the spot... But, well, they all seemed to be happy about it, so I was just glad they liked it.

After all that, the only thing left was the final words from the bride and groom.

As they stepped up to the stage, I cast [**Speaker**] on them one more time.

"Everyone... Today, we've taken the first step in our new life together. I'm thankful beyond words for all your blessings and words of celebration. To be honest, I am still inexperienced in many ways, but I would be extremely glad for you to continue to support us as we set off down a new path together. Thank you all, every one of you here!" A warm applause followed as the bride and groom bowed up on the stage before all those present.

"Once the ceremony is over, the grand duke of Brunhild himself has privately reserved his game room for us! To all those present who have no pressing matters to attend to, I extend an invitation to you all to join us there if you would like!" The entire crowd raised their voices in excitement and anticipation. From there, I cast a [Gate] and fixed the location to the game room in my castle in Brunhild.

In the game room, the Blitz family maid and the Strand family employees had come to provide assistance for the guests.

They had already prepared mountains of food and drinks on the tables for all the guests, in preparation for the afterparty.

Normally the afterparty of a wedding would only include close friends and relatives and the like... Although I'd already learned time and again that relying on common sense from my old world was useless over here.

"Oho. So this is Brunhild's rumored game room, is it?"

"There are many things of great interest all around me. Truly a fascinating place." And so, the bride and groom's parents came to join in the afterparty.

General Leon looked ready to play until he collapsed, meanwhile Olba's instincts as a merchant were thrown into overdrive at the sight of it all.

What followed was an explosion of merrymaking hijinks as everyone present ran around having the time of their lives. Between all the drunken antics and folks playing games, the whole place was as lively as it ever could have been.

After a while, a number of guests left for home through my [Gate]. Most of them were young women. As they were leaving, a number of men came forward saying that they would 'escort the ladies home.' One such man was Shyon — Lyon's older brother — who came forward to escort a particularly beautiful young lady home. He was a smooth player.

As the clock struck ten, the bride and groom decided to rest for the night. I had already prepared a guest room for them further away in the other end of the castle. It was the first night of their marriage, so, well, even I knew the implications of what came next. A number of the guests wished to spend the night in the castle, too, so I directed them to a different area of guest rooms. Naturally, aside from family members and married couples, I made sure that the men and women's guest rooms were set apart from each other for obvious reasons.

After partying well into the early hours of the morning, a number of the guests woke up with hangovers. I had made a tactical retreat the moment I saw my chance, but apparently General Leon and Olba had kept drinking with each other for the longest time, until they retreated to their own guest rooms where they immediately collapsed into their beds and fell asleep in no time at all. Lyon and his new wife left early in the morning to their family home. I wished them well.

It was a tense time setting it all up, but it all worked out. After a while, I was surprised to learn that a trend in Belfast began where people partied far into the night and had fun after a wedding.

"Let us deepen our love."

"Come again?" I froze at Yumina's sudden exclamation. What in the world was she thinking, saying something like that out of nowhere? I would've at least liked to eat my breakfast in peace and quiet for once.

"The thought came to me after seeing that wedding ceremony the other day. I would like our wedding to be just as beautiful and display our overflowing love for each other. For that, I believe we need to get to know each other better, connect with each other on a deeper emotional level, and deepen our love for each other." In contrast to Yumina whose eyes were sparkling with a spellbound gaze, all I could do was give my best effort to return her gaze with a forced smile. I understood what she was saying, and I also believed that it was an important step in furthering our relationship, but, well, my embarrassment was the foremost emotion that seized me in that moment.

Ignoring my feelings completely, a certain person leaped up from their chair at the dining table. That person was none other than Lu.

"A wonderful idea, Yumina! I had been thinking the same for the longest time! We really must deepen our bonds of love with Touya!"

"Exactly!"

"Indeed!" The two princesses leaped up and embraced each other in their mutual understanding. It should, by all rights, have been a charming scene to watch, but something about the whole situation made me feel very anxious and uneasy.

"Err... What, exactly, did you have in mind?" Linze, her face completely red, inquired this of Yumina, while keeping her gaze locked onto me. Elze and Yae had both stopped eating their meals partway through and were also gazing over at the princesses.

"Why, a date, of course!"

"A *date*?! I know of dates! It's where a man and a woman who are close to each other go around many places outside together!"

"That's right. It mainly involves going around having meals together, going shopping together, watching plays in theaters together and such. By which it's an event which deepens the intimacy and emotional bonds of those who are on the date together." Yumina gave the excited Lu a brief explanation of what a date would entail.

Deepen our intimacy...? I mean, I'm already engaged to everyone, so I don't really know if a date's gonna do anything to deepen our intimacy any more than it already is.

"As a matter of fact, Touya has been neglecting us far too much lately. Are you that type of person? The kind of man who would catch and keep a fish without ever feeding it?"

"Erk..."

"I-I feel the same! Like yesterday, I didn't get to see Touya even once after we'd finished our breakfast meals."

"I, too. That is... I have been feeling rather... Lonely, lately... I have." Urk. It was true that I'd been running around all over the place doing this and that, not having much time to spend with the girls. I felt like I should reflect on that and try to make it up to them somehow.

It may very well have been true that I'd been taking advantage of their good will and running off doing my own things instead. Still, I did love these girls. I wanted to be with them forever, and I wanted to make them all as happy as I possibly could. In spite of that, I hadn't been putting in enough effort for that.

Still, a date? A date... Even if we went on one, there still weren't many places in Brunhild where we could go out and enjoy ourselves on a date... I could take them to the Silver Moon Inn, or a cafe somewhere, but that was about all I could think of on that front.

As for clothes shopping, there was always Zanac's store or Olba's Company.

Even if we went shopping, we could only really visit three or four stores. Would they really be satisfied with just that?

"It's a bit more than just that. I want to go out with Touya, and make precious memories together so that one day, when we're older, we can happily look back on those memories, on things like 'We did do something like that, didn't we?' or 'Something like that did happen, didn't it?', and I want to be able to reminisce about such things with Touya as we grow older and older and make more and more wonderful memories together." That was right… Yumina was absolutely right. Besides, my [Gate] wasn't just limited to Brunhild, it could take us just about anywhere we wanted now, be it other countries or wherever. If I didn't make use of that ability now, then when would I?

"…Alright, then how about this. For today, we'll all go out together on a date. We'll visit lots of places and do a whole bunch of fun things together." The moment I spoke those words, everyone's faces lit up in smiles. In that very moment, I decided I wanted to protect those smiles forever.

"Now that that's decided, we must make suitable preparations!" Lu's announcement seemed to have flipped a switch in everyone, as they began devouring their breakfast at an amazing speed before clearing away their plates and heading straight back to their own rooms. I could understand that they were excited about it, but if you eat your breakfast that fast it could be bad for your digestive system.

As for me, I went to visit Kousaka to let him know that I had to change our planned schedule to another day as an important matter had come up. Fortunately, the work we'd had planned only involved things like marking the districts of the town and inspecting land that could be used for farming, so I figured it should be fine.

I sat out on the terrace enjoying the wonderful tea that our butler Laim had prepared as I waited for the girls, when suddenly I heard a stampede of footsteps heading right in my direction.

"Sorry for the wait."

"…" Gazing upon the sight of the girls before me, I very nearly spilled my tea everywhere.

Everyone's outfits were drastically different than usual.

Yumina was dressed in a cardigan with a large collar, a tiered skirt, and black tights.

Lu wore a jumper skirt, and a blouse with a ribbon on the front.

Elze had decided to go with a blouse, with a long, knitted cardigan over it, as well as a culotte skirt and black tights.

Now Linze, she had gone with a classic dress with an embroidered flower pattern around the collar, wearing a cardigan over the top, and kneesocks for her legs.

Amongst all of this, Yae's outfit was the one that surprised me the most. She kept her ponytail as it was, but she wasn't in her usual hakama, or in fact any Eashen clothing at all — Yae was outfitted in a hooded blouson jacket and knee-length trousers. She wasn't wearing her usual zouri either, but rather fashionable shoes instead.

None of their outfits looked like fashion that was common in this world at all.

"Those clothes…"

"We each had Zanac make them for us specifically for this sort of occasion. We ordered them specially once we learned that you'd come up with the designs for them, Touya." I certainly had given such clothing designs to Zanac by way of my [**Drawing**] skill, but I honestly hadn't expected the debut of those designs to happen like this.

241

"So… H-How do I look?"

"Eh? Ah, yeah. You look really beautiful. Those outfits actually look really great on all of you. They really suit you." Elze asked me while blushing, and I just answered reflexively. But it was true that I thought they all looked really cute in those clothes. I never would've thought that a simple change of clothes would leave such a deep impression on me.

"Well then, let us depart on our date! Oh, but before that…" As if taking the lead for something, Lu turned to face the other girls and clenched her fist.

Following her lead, the rest of the girls also each clenched one of their fists with a sharp look in their eyes.

"Rock, paper… Scissors!"

"That was a draw, so… Go!"

Umm… What exactly are you refined ladies up to, playing rock-paper-scissors…?

"I have won!"

"I-I won, too!" It seemed like Lu and Linze had won at something, but… What was this all about? Just as I was wondering that, the answer came to me without warning. Rushing up to my side, Lu and Linze each wrapped themselves around my arms.

"Just remember that we're going to be switching after a while, you two."

"Such regret, regret indeed…"

"Hey! Aren't you clinging to him a bit too much?!"

Oh, now I get it. Hrmm… On the one hand this is a very pleasurable experience, but on the other, it's pretty damn embarrassing… Meanwhile, Laim was laughing at the sight. Yup, definitely pretty embarrassing…

I somehow managed to convince the two ladies to just link arms with me instead. It was still embarrassing, but it was better than having them wrapping their entire bodies around me in public. Though I'd be lying if I said it wasn't a pleasant experience either way.

"Now, where should we go first?"

"Let us visit Refreese first! I have never been there before, and I would like to see it at least once."

"Alright, if that's what you want. Refreese will be our first stop, then." Everyone was on board with Lu's suggestion, so I whipped up a [Gate] to Refreese's Imperial City, Bern.

Bern was a beautiful scenic city surrounded by wonderful sights of nature. It resembled the towns of Santorini with their overlooking view of the Aegean Sea, as the blue of the sea and the sky merged together into the horizon blending together into a single world of blue. The white walls of the stores and buildings of the street on the hill road only helped to enhance the beauty of the scenery.

Perhaps it was because we were in a high place, but we were embraced by a gentle and refreshing breeze.

"What a lovely city this is!"

"The breeze is so refreshing, it is~" Being their first trip to Bern, Lu and Yae were enraptured by the wonder of the beautiful scenery around them.

Yumina had apparently been here a few times with her family due to royal affairs, meanwhile Elze and Linze were born and raised in Refreese. I'd heard from them that they'd been to the Imperial City a couple of times before. After admiring the scenery, next we took off to go wander around the fancy accessory shops and general goods stores in Bern, enjoying our little shopping trip.

When all five of the girls asked me to pick out something that suited each of them, I at first struggled to think of what would be

244

best for each of them. After a lot of thought, I went for a selection of five brooches, each styled after the design of the flower that best suited each girl, and gave them to the girls as gifts.

I also picked up a few souvenirs for the people back at the castle. They were always helping me and looking out for me, so I wanted to thank them in some way. I hoped they'd be happy with what I got for them.

Our next stop was a cafe at the top of a small hill, where we decided to have a bite to eat. Apparently the time to switch had come, so now Yumina and Elze were linking arms with me.

Assaulted by their "Say aaah" attacks as they fed me by spoon, my shyness began to reach critical levels. Yumina was pulling off this advanced move like it was nothing, while Elze on the other hand let out her little "S-Say aaahhn" attack while blushing to her ears.

God dammit, why are you so cute, you little rascal?!

"Wherever are we going next, then?" Yae asked as she took my arm. Lu had taken my other arm once more.

"Ah, Touya, look! It seems like there's a theatre troupe putting on a display down in the town plaza." Yumina pointed to a poster on the wall. It was an advertisement by a theatre troupe for a play called "Bakram the Mighty Dragon Slayer." By the title alone, it didn't feel like the kind of performance you'd usually go to watch while on a date.

"Bakram the Mighty Dragon Slayer is a love story about a certain woman. In order to gain approval for the marriage of her beloved, she goes on a quest to fight an Evil Dragon, but the Dragon..."

"STOP! If you spoil the story, it won't be nearly as interesting to watch!" As the older sister, Elze stopped Linze before her explanation went into spoiler territory. *Still, a love story, eh?* If that was the case, maybe everyone would enjoy seeing it, after all.

"So, you wanna go see it?"

"Yes!" Right as we were about to head to the location of the plaza listed on the poster, our path was blocked by four men.

"Yo, buddy. Popular guy, ain't ya? Makes me real jealous, y'get what I mean?" One of the men called out to me with a vulgar smile staining his face. The guys were all dressed like adventurers, but not a single one of them seemed to have any decent equipment on them at all. If anything, they just looked like a group of halfwit thugs. They didn't even look that much older than me. Though in this world, that was still old enough to be considered an adult.

"Do you have some business with me?"

"Nah, nothin' that important. Y'see, we ain't got much cash right now. Then we come across a dude who's trailin' a bunch of women all wrapped 'round his arms, an' we figured y'might be able to spot us some cash with the virtue of that wide ol' heart a' yours. Get it?" So they were just decorating extortion in pretty words. It was a sad sight to see such human trash loitering around in such a beautiful city. The emperor sure must have his hands full already, and now this…

"Look, buddy, don't you think it's a bit shameful to be trying to extort money, even from a guy like me? You're old enough to be responsible for your own livelihood, so just go out and get a job like everyone else."

"The fuck you say?! Look, brat, d'ya even get what's goin' on here?!"

"We ain't lookin' for a priest, we're lookin' for a profit. Now hand over yer wallet if ya know what's good for ya."

"Hell, if ya ain't gonna hand over yer wallet, we'd be fine takin' them girlies ye've got with ya. We'll make sure to take *reeeaaal* good care of 'em in yer place." The thugs all burst out into a vulgar display of laughter.

One of them reached out his hand toward Lu, so I figured I should at least give him one good punch to set him straight and took a step forward. But before I could do anything, two people made their move before I could.

"Gnuogh?!"

"Ahgyaaagh!" Yae grabbed the laughing thug by the wrist and threw him straight down onto the ground.

Elze swept the legs of another one of the thugs and then sent him flying.

"Wh-Whaddya think you're doin' you bitch?!"

"I don't want to waste my precious time dealing with human garbage like you. Would you get the hell out of my sight, right this instant?"

"I very much agree, I do. I very much would not care to dirty our precious day dealing with the likes of you, I would not." Elze and Yae shot the thugs a glare so cold it could freeze the very air itself.

When I glanced to my side, I noticed that Lu, Yumina, and Linze were all shooting the same ice-cold glare at them. The atmosphere was so tense I could barely move. My instincts were telling me that the girls were even sending *me* the message "Don't you dare lift a finger here."

"Crazy bitches, don't fuck with us! Ya'd best be ready now that ye've done that to us!" The two thugs that had been knocked down stood back up, and the whole gang whipped out knives from their pockets. They must've thought we'd be easy to take down, judging by the disgusting smiles on their faces.

"They must surely believe that they could intimidate us if they came at us in a group all armed with knives, I suspect."

"I suppose I should have expected this. They truly are little more than a group of petty thugs."

"They're the textbook example of utter lowlifes." These girls weren't holding anything back...

"ORAAH!" One of the men Linze had called a lowlife charged straight for Elze, knife in hand and ready to stab her. Naturally, Elze wasn't about to be taken down by a puny thug like this. There was a dry cracking sound as Elze shattered the hand the man was holding the knife in, and in the same movement she brought her heel crashing down against the back of the man's head.

"Guhhuergh?!"

"You bitch... Guahberagh?!" A second man charged at Elze from behind, only to be knocked out in one shot by Elze's roundhouse kick.

Another charged at Yae, who swiftly dodged the man's knife, grabbed him by the arm, and slammed him against the wall in a single swift movement.

The last man standing looked at Yae and Elze like his brain couldn't even process what had just happened.

"Y-You bastards! I'll get you for this! You'd better remember that!" Abandoning his companions, the man ran away in such a rush that he tripped over several times as he fled.

"As if we'd bother to remember a lowlife like that."

"Everything from the way he ran away to the line he left us with merely proves his status as a mere thug."

"He got... everything that he deserved." They really were running their mouths off here...

"Elze, Yae, are you alright?"

"As if I'd ever get hurt against an opponent like *that*."

"Goodness sake… It appears that fools like them can be found in any country, they can." Yae remarked as she observed the three men collapsed before her. There was some truth to her words, though. On rare occasions, thugs like that even popped up in Brunhild sometimes.

"You fellas are pretty strong, huh? But you'd best be careful. They're part of a group of scoundrels who've claimed this area as their territory. Their leader's a bit of an infamous big-shot, almost worse than the actual criminals around here. My advice? You should probably get out of here as soon as you can." A kind old man who'd watched our little conflict gave us a concerned warning. The fact that these thugs had their own territory was bad enough already. Disorder among the public leads to disorder among the whole country. *Next time I see His Imperial Presence, I'll need to give him a strict talking to.*

"Alright, let's forget about all this nonsense and get going. Wouldn't want to miss the play." Elze grabbed me by the arm and took off running. I struggled to match her pace for a moment there.

"Hold it right there, Elze! It is my turn to take Touya's arm!"

"It is my turn too, it is!" Everyone began chasing after the two of us as we dashed down the hill. Lu and Yae were shouting out complaints, but they still seemed to be having great fun with it all.

We joked around with our mock-complaints and little arguments in a way so as not to cause any public disturbance, as we entered the tent where the theater troupe was putting on their play.

"That was pretty interesting!"

"Yeah, both the acting and the script were great."

"Bakram the Dragon Slayer" was quite an interesting play. It started out as a simple love story, but as the tale progressed, political intrigue, love rivals, and Dragons all made an appearance. It was a gripping production that spanned four acts.

Best of all, this wasn't fiction. Apparently the play was based off a true story from a hundred years ago. Of course, certain parts had likely been embellished for dramatic effect.

"Maybe we should invite a troupe like that to our country sometime."

"I don't see why not. I'm sure everyone would be happy." Chatting excitedly, we made our way to the restaurant that'd recently become the talk of the city in Refreese. According to Yumina's sources, even the reclusive princess has snuck out of the castle before to go eat there. *I really hope we don't end up running into her...*

After a few minutes of walking, Yae and Elze sidle up to me and surreptitiously whisper into my ear.

"We're being tailed."

"I knew it." A while back I'd noticed a group tracking us.

"There's six to our right, five to our left and eight behind us... I believe that's all."

"That's quite the force. What do you imagine their objective is?" I casually glanced to my right. The figures instantly retreated into the shadows, but before they vanished I distinctly made out one of the thugs we'd ran into earlier.

"I guess he brought his cronies along to try and teach us a lesson."

"Aaah, I see now."

Elze heaved a sigh as understanding dawned on her. Yae slipped back and informed the other three of the situation.

"How unpleasant..."

"Some people never learn I suppose."

"Sheesh, what a pain." I could feel the girls' wrath flare up. The heat was almost palpable. Well, I understood their anger. To be honest, I was rather frustrated myself. They were interrupting my precious quality time with everyone.

I could have just locked on to all of them and hit them with [Paralyze], but then they might have come after me again. It would be best to put an end to this once and for all.

"It's not so bad to get some exercise before dinner, right?"

"I doubt we'll manage to even work up a sweat… It's obvious those thugs won't put up a decent fight." I made small talk with Elze as I lured the thugs into a deserted alleyway. The sun was just beginning to set, and the sky was a fiery red.

I was hoping to settle things before night fell.

"This should be good enough." We stopped at an empty street. Seeing their chance, the thugs trickled out from behind the cover of nearby buildings. They were carrying crude cudgels in their hands. Two, four, six… more than I'd thought. Less than thirty though.

"They's the ones, boss!"

"Oh, pretty little things, ain't they? This should be fun." The thug from earlier had brought over a hulking bear of a man. He had a knife in his hand, and a longsword strapped to his waist. So this guy was the Big Boss of the little ruffian gang, huh. Well, whatever.

Fitting of a boss of a group of trash, the boss himself had quite the crooked-looking face with his perverted grin.

"Yer luck ran out when you made an enemy of us, fellas. Oy, you there. Yeah, you, the brat. If ya leave all the cash you've got on ya and hand over the women, I might even consider lettin' ya go free."

"Dumbass." I whipped out my Brunhild gun and shot the leader right in the temple with a rubber bullet. Knocked back by the force of the sudden attack, he fell backward and collapsed to the ground unconscious. I wasn't about to just stand and wait for an enemy armed with a weapon to come charging at me.

"B-Boooss?!"

"Y-You bastards, the fuck d'ya think you're doin'?! Guys, go get 'im—"

"Blow forth, Wind: Soaring, Spinning Gust: [Whirlwind]!"

"Uwoooooaaahhh!" A burst of wind came out of nowhere and sent a number of the thugs flying into the air. As expected of Yumina, skilled as ever.

"Entwine thus, Ice! Frozen Curse: [Icebind]!"

"Nuoouh?! M-My feet are frozen?!" This time Linze showed off her magic skills by freezing one of the thugs' shoes to the ground. Normally that spell was meant to freeze the legs completely, meaning Linze had deliberately held back.

Following up Linze's move, Elze moved in with a straight punch of considerable force, sending the thug flying through the air so hard that he was blown right out of his shoes still frozen to the ground.

"Gnuhuoh?!"

"Ouhgack?!" Apparently Lu had snatched one of the enemy's weapons before anyone could even notice, and was striking down thug after thug with a simple wooden stick.

"Lu-dono's skill is rather impressive, it is. I suppose it is time for my turn, then." Yae swiftly snatched a length of timber from one of the thugs and struck one of them heavily right on the shoulder. With her improvised weapon, she continued to send anyone who came her way flat to the ground face-first with great skill.

After just a single minute had passed, roughly thirty or so thugs were all down and collapsed in the alleyway.

"Well, then." Using **[Power Rise]**, I gathered the entire group of thugs into one big pile. I took a piece of paper and wrote "These men are a group of bandits and robbers. I have therefore taken the liberty of arresting them." and slapped the note on the leader of the group.

Having done this, I opened up a [Gate] to the Refreese Knight's patrol station that I'd seen near the theater tent and lugged the lot of them through it. That took care of that.

"Honestly… Now our precious date has been completely ruined." Yumina puffed out her cheeks in dissatisfaction, and I did my best to calm her down. She was cute when she was angry, but I still wanted the girls I loved to be smiling as often as possible.

"C'mon Yumina, we can all just visit anywhere at any time. We're going to be together for the rest of our lives, after all. We'll have plenty of chances to go on dates. In a few years, we might even look back on this little incident as a funny memory. To be honest, I still really had a lot of fun with our date today."

"Touya…"

"Hey, don't just casually say it like our date's already over! We've still got plenty of time to go out and have even more fun!"

"Very true, indeed."

"Precisely! Now, let us all head off to a restaurant!"

"I'm, looking forward to that."

"Hey, don't drag me along like that! The restaurant's not gonna get up and run away, you know!" As the sun set on our date and the stars in the sky shone above us, we, all of us, all ran together under the starlit sky.

The food in the restaurant was delicious. It was so good that I couldn't have been more satisfied. Everyone had returned to their usual cheerful selves, too. We managed to end our hectic date on a very positive note.

When we returned to the castle, I handed out the souvenirs that I'd bought for everyone. I took a bath and went to my room to retire for the night, only for that thought to be interrupted by a certain group of five girls in their pajamas who had barged right into my bedroom, leaving me at a complete loss.

Just for the record, nothing indecent happened between us at all. The five had fallen right asleep in my bed leaving little room for me, so I had no choice but to sleep on the couch for the night. Still, all in all, it had been a wonderful day.

I told myself that I'd do my best tomorrow, too.

Hello there. It's me, Patora Fuyuhara.

We've finally released the fifth volume of In Another World With My Smartphone.

Thanks again for sticking with me this far. I hope you continue to enjoy my work.

In the last volume, Touya became the ruler of a country, and he's now the grand duke of Brunhild.

From here, the story will become about Touya's journey across the world, using his duchy as a home base.

He has a home now, so he won't be lugging around so much dead weight. Plus, he has alliances with the surrounding nations, so they'll help him if he encounters trouble, and vice versa.

Going forward, the story will see Touya traveling to various countries with his entourage, solving various confrontations. Don't expect it to mix up too heavily just yet, though.

In Another World With My Smartphone was written to be an easy-going, comfy adventure, after all.

In this volume, Pam uses a pretty basic syllable-based language. I toyed around with the idea of making her speak in symbols like ★ %☆■○◆*, but I thought that might be a little boring.

In the end, it doesn't really matter if you can't understand what she's saying. There's no hidden story in her lines or anything, so it's fine.

I wrote a bit about a wedding in this volume, did you know I used to work for a place that held weddings?

The only issue is, the place held weddings in Hall A, and... funerals in Hall B. There were a few times where I got the two places mixed up, and there was one particular incident where I nearly rushed into the middle of a funeral to deliver a "congratulations" card... That would've been dangerous, for sure...

Alright, it's time to give my thanks as usual.

Eiji Usatsuka, thank you again for your illustrations. I really liked the pictures in this volume, they're just so lovely. I've seen the ones for the next volume, and they're amazing too!

K. As usual, thank you so much. Sorry if I'm ever a burden. I'm looking forward to working with you more in the future.

To everyone at Hobby Japan's editorial department, please take my most sincere thanks.

And once again, to all of those who supported me on "Shousetsuka ni Narou," you have my gratitude.

Ohoho, I am excited though, because next volume we're finally going to include *that* in the story... I really can't wait, I hope you all enjoy where the plot goes from here.

Well then, dear readers. I'm looking forward to speaking with you in volume six. See you then.

— Patora Fuyuhara

Patora Fuyuhara
illustration: Eiji Usatsuka

Another World With My Smartphone

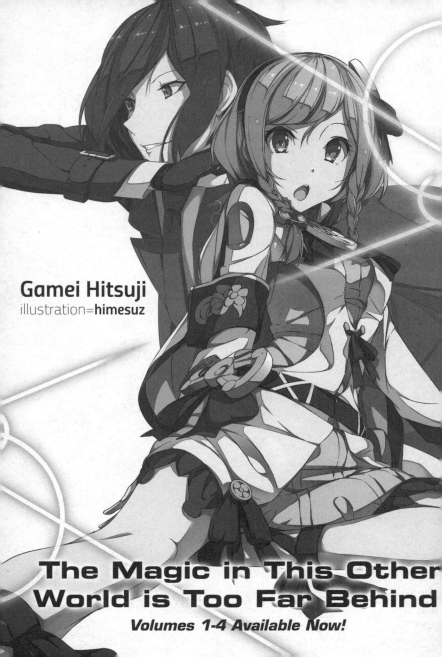

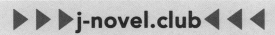

J-Novel Club Lineup

Ebook Releases Series List

Amagi Brilliant Park
An Archdemon's Dilemma: How to Love Your Elf Bride
Ao Oni
Arifureta Zero
Arifureta: From Commonplace to World's Strongest
Bluesteel Blasphemer
Brave Chronicle: The Ruinmaker
Clockwork Planet
Demon King Daimaou
Der Werwolf: The Annals of Veight
ECHO
From Truant to Anime Screenwriter: My Path to "Anohana" and "The Anthem of the Heart"
Gear Drive
Grimgar of Fantasy and Ash
How a Realist Hero Rebuilt the Kingdom
How NOT to Summon a Demon Lord
I Saved Too Many Girls and Caused the Apocalypse
If It's for My Daughter, I'd Even Defeat a Demon Lord
In Another World With My Smartphone
Infinite Dendrogram
Infinite Stratos
Invaders of the Rokujouma!?
JK Haru is a Sex Worker in Another World
Kokoro Connect
Last and First Idol
Lazy Dungeon Master
Me, a Genius? I Was Reborn into Another World and I Think They've Got the Wrong Idea!
Mixed Bathing in Another Dimension
My Big Sister Lives in a Fantasy World
My Little Sister Can Read Kanji
My Next Life as a Villainess: All Routes Lead to Doom!
Occultic;Nine
Outbreak Company
Paying to Win in a VRMMO
Seirei Gensouki: Spirit Chronicles
Sorcerous Stabber Orphen: The Wayward Journey
The Faraway Paladin
The Magic in this Other World is Too Far Behind!
The Master of Ragnarok & Blesser of Einherjar
The Unwanted Undead Adventurer
Walking My Second Path in Life
Yume Nikki: I Am Not in Your Dream